Utah Thirteeners

Utah Thirteeners

A GUIDE TO CLIMBING THE 13,000-FOOT PEAKS OF THE HIGH UINTAS

David Rose

THE UNIVERSITY OF UTAH PRESS

Salt Lake City

Warning: Climbing and hiking the Uinta Mountains are inherently dangerous. The Uintas are subject to dynamic natural forces, including sudden changes in weather and route conditions. Your safety depends on your own judgment and decision-making abilities. If you have any doubt as to your ability to do any of the routes described in this book, do not attempt them. Neither the author nor the publisher assumes any liability for injury, damage to property, or violation of the law that may arise from the usage of this book.

Use of this book indicates the reader's assumption that it may contain errors, as well as acknowledgment that the user is solely responsible for his or her own abilities to climb and hike in a safe and responsible manner.

 The Defiance House Man colophon is a registered trademark of the University of Utah Press. It is based upon a four-foot-tall, Ancient Puebloan pictograph (late PIII) near Glen Canyon, Utah.

LIBRARY OF CONGRESS CATALOGING-IN-PUBLICATION DATA

Rose, David.

Utah thirteeners : a guide to climbing the 13,000-foot peaks of the high Uintas / David Rose.

    p. cm.

  ISBN 0-87480-794-8 (pbk. : alk. paper)

  1. Mountaineering—Uinta Mountains (Utah and Wyo.)—Guidebooks. 2. Trails—Uinta Mountains (Utah and Wyo.)—Guidebooks. 3. Uinta Mountains (Utah and Wyo.)—Maps. 4. Uinta Mountains (Utah and Wyo.)—Guidebooks. I. Title.

  GV199.42.U36R67 2004

  796.52'2'0979214—dc22

2003027559

CONTENTS

MAPS

PEAK CHECKLIST

	Rank	Peak	Elevation (feet)
☐	1	Kings Peak	13,528
☐	2	South Kings Peak	13,512
☐	3	Gilbert Peak	13,442
☐	4	Mount Emmons	13,440
☐	5	First Gemini (AN)	13,387
☐	6	Second Gemini (AN)	13,306
☐	7	Pyramid Peak (AN)	13,287
☐	8	Gunsight Peak (AN)	13,263
☐	9	Fortress Peak (AN)	13,260
☐	10	Ramp Peak (AN)	13,247
☐	11	Mount Lovenia	13,219
☐	12	Glacier Peak (AN)	13,170
☐	13	Tokewanna Peak	13,165
☐	14	Mount Powell	13,159
☐	15	Wasatch Peak	13,156
☐	16	Dome Peak (AN)	13,103
☐	17	Pinnacle Peak (AN)	13,068
☐	18	Cliff Point (AN)	13,064
☐	19	Wilson Peak	13,055
☐	20	Mount Wapiti (AN)	13,039
☐	21	Quandary Peak (AN)	13,032

AN = author's name

PREFACE

My first Uinta summit was Kings Peak. I climbed it simply because it was the highest point in Utah, oblivious to any 13,000-foot-peak list, or any high-point list, for that matter. My interest in high points came later, after reading a newspaper article about a man who was climbing the highest points in the fifty states (at the time a relatively uncommon thing to attempt), and who had a collection of summit rocks in his office, one from each peak. From this article, I came up with a more accessible goal: climbing the highest peaks in every county in Utah, which I began in 1989. While I was working on the list, newspaper articles and guidebooks like *High in Utah* detailing the county peaks appeared, a confirmation to me of the growing popularity and attraction of climbing high points of all kinds.

During that same time I'd been backpacking frequently in the Uintas, and had begun climbing a group of 13,000-foot summits briefly listed in Michael Kelsey's *Utah Mountaineering Guide.* After climbing them all over the course of several years, it struck me that these "Utah 13ers" were a natural addition to any high-point list, and that there was a need for a dedicated guidebook with more detailed information. Colorado and California have various guides to both the 14ers and the 13ers—why not Utah? The book was in my mind for more than a year, while a friend, Valerie Clark, kept nudging me to get started. I made a proposal to Jeff Grathwohl at the University of Utah Press, and he liked the idea. Not having climbed the peaks the first time with a guidebook in mind, I climbed them again in several intense trips, and later made additional trips to do alternative routes. It would be hard to come up with a better excuse for getting into the mountains than the need to "research" a guidebook!

There's something very satisfying about climbing high points, of achieving a goal on your own terms, under your own power. Some people view such "peak bagging" as a superficial outdoor activity. In my mind, high-point climbing fits perfectly into the bigger picture of enjoying nature and the backcountry, particularly with peaks like the 13ers that require relatively long hikes into remote wilderness. I've had incredible experiences hiking and peak climbing in the Uintas: adventuresome ridges and boulder scrambles, sweeping mountain vistas, snowfield glissades, crisp September days and frosty starfilled nights, thunderstorms, snowstorms, rainbows, rutting moose, elk herds, wildflowers, lush meadows...the list goes on. I hope you find climbing the Uinta 13ers as fulfilling as I have.

Utah Thirteeners

INTRODUCTION

This book will guide you to the roof of Utah: twenty-one high and wild mountain summits above 13,000 feet, all positioned in the heart of the High Uintas Wilderness Area. To climb these peaks is to have a wilderness summit experience unequaled anywhere else in the state. All the routes described are summer-season nontechnical hikes or scrambles—doable by most moderately experienced hikers.

If you're a high-points climber, the challenge is natural—the 13ers are another goal to add to your ventures. But anyone—high-point enthusiast or not—attempting the 13ers will enjoy a refreshing new look at the range. The 13ers aren't always the most popular or prominent peaks, so you'll end up discovering some fantastic mountains you otherwise might have overlooked. Climbers swarm Kings Peak, yet other summits (particularly the unnamed 13ers) are equally rewarding but relatively ignored.

You'll get away from the masses fishing the lakes and hiking the trails below (and getting eaten by mosquitoes), and enjoy solitary views of the Uintas from the high perspective of the climber, a world that most people will never see. The mountain vistas from atop Utah's highest places are inspiring and incredible. The high, rocky ridges that contain the summits are almost a separate world within the Uinta range, a realm of gargantuan boulder fields, a few hardy plants and flowers, harsh weather, snowfields, and tremendous views. It may be tempting to stay in basins, but once you are up there, climbing higher, the exhilaration of the summit gets to you (and is even addictive!).

The setting of the 13ers in the glorious High Uintas Wilderness Area enhances the peak-climbing experience. It's not just any wilderness; it's Utah's largest and most wild, and you can drive only so far before you must put on a backpack and start hiking. Virtually all other major peaks scattered throughout Utah can be climbed in a day from where you park your car. For the average person, summer 13er climbs will take more than one day (unless you're capable of doing more than twenty miles in a day), especially factoring in driving time to get to the trailheads. This larger time commitment keeps weekend crowding to a minimum. The heaviest usage in the Uintas is within a day's hike of the trailhead, so you can enjoy increasing solitude as you hike toward the

13ers, especially once leaving the trail for the summits. As well, vistas and geology change rapidly the higher you ascend; as a Uinta mountain climber, you'll get to see it all, from bottom to top. I for one am happy the summits aren't more "convenient"—if they were, you might have views of civilization instead of wild panoramas.

Although there are hundreds of miles of maintained trails crisscrossing the Uintas, no 13er has a maintained trail to the top, I'm glad to say. Except for Kings Peak, there aren't even worn paths to establish a common route. However, the routes are generally obvious, and none of them requires technical climbing, just plenty of stamina and boulder-negotiation ability. You'll quickly learn the art of constant "boulder-hopping." Many routes could be considered "hikes," the rest of them "scrambles" of various levels. No ropes or rock climbing are necessary, and the route descriptions actually assume you will be going in the mostly snow-free seasons of summer and fall. Even if you wanted to rock climb, the Uintas in general have very few good technical rock-climbing routes. Any slopes steep enough for ropes generally have so much loose rock that it's at least unpleasant if not completely unsafe—often making the easier routes the most logical and prudent choices for hikers of any skill level.

Adding to the challenge of the relatively long approach trails and boulder-covered summits is the high altitude. The Uinta Mountains as a whole (summits as well as basin trails) are remarkably higher than any other area of the state. In fact, most routes in this book start at 11,000 feet, almost equal to the highest elevation of much of the Wasatch Range. The high altitude affects not only your lungs, but also the weather. Temperatures are lower than surrounding land, and regular precipitation is the norm. Thus, planning for and around inclement weather is a part of every Uinta trip.

The twenty-one summits are divided into four main Groups (specified with a capital *G* throughout this book) according to trailhead access and proximity to each other. Within each Group, you'll find excellent route alternatives for any single peak, but with an emphasis on the best ways to climb them in combinations (that is, multipeak routes from a base camp). The introduction to each Group briefly explains the one-day route possibilities. If you're a dedicated high-points climber, you'll be happy to know that it's possible to climb all the peaks in any given group in one short "peak-bagging" backpacking trip (lasting three to six days) from a single trailhead, weather permitting.

Doing more than one Uinta summit in the same day requires a certain level of endurance but isn't nearly as crazy as it might sound. Often, the routes leave from high passes accessed by trails, and the 13ers are positioned relatively close together, so climbing them in groups is very natural. Many times the hardest

Island Lake, Henrys Fork basin

part is getting to the high ridge tops; continuing along the ridge to the next peak is relatively quick and takes less energy than descending to base camp and climbing back up again the next day. For some peaks, the best route requires going over another 13er anyway. The routes are only suggestions—they are segmented by peak so you can, to a certain extent, divide the summits into separate trips as you see fit.

About the Summit List

While this book describes twenty-one summits, the number isn't all that concrete. It hinges on the actual definition of a "peak." Such definitions have always been debated among mountaineers. In Colorado, for instance, the number of peaks classified as 14ers has varied between fifty-two and fifty-five over the years, depending on the formula used. The only final answer is that every mountain region is unique and has its own rules that make sense for that region.

Twelve of the twenty-one summits don't have official names. There is a tendency to attach more prestige and meaning to named mountain peaks. In my opinion, the lack of given names is an attraction, a testament to the peaks' remoteness and wildness. To make the summits easier to describe (rather than having twelve peaks listed as "Unnamed"), I refer to them by my own suggested names.

Quadrangles (7.5", 1:24,000) of the Uintas actually show twenty-five points above 13,000 feet. Nineteen of them are clearly distinct mountain peaks (versus spurs or ridge bumps). The remaining six high points are questionable. They include three of the four points of Mount Powell, Cliff Point (the point west of Fortress Peak), the point north of South Kings Peak, and one of the Geminis. I decided to include Cliff Point and both Geminis in the 13ers list based on the "distance factor." That is, the greater the distance between the questionable point and the nearest definite 13er, the more likely it is that the questionable point could be defined as a separate peak and not just a high ridge-top point. The two greatest of such distances are Cliff Point to Fortress Peak (a definite 13er) and Second Gemini to First Gemini (a definite 13er). Regardless of which of the twenty-five summits or points made "the list," the routes in this book will actually lead you to (or over) all of them.

Two 13ers don't have elevations printed on topographic maps: Wilson Peak and Fortress Peak. For these peaks I used a combination of topographic-map software, contour-line spacing, and my knowledge of the actual physical characteristics of the summit to come up with my estimated elevations. Fortress Peak's actual height could very well be higher than Gunsight Peak, but I've placed it slightly lower because Gunsight does have an official elevation. But the "real" elevation of these two summits doesn't ultimately matter—the only difference an elevation change could make is their order in the list; they are both definitely 13ers.

Finally, it is interesting to note that most of the 13er list remains intact even when using a neatly rounded number in the metric system. The metric number that approximately corresponds to 13,000 feet is 4,000 meters (13,123 feet). Creating such a 4,000-meter-summit list drops the list to fifteen, Wasatch Peak being the fifteenth. Wilson Peak is the only officially named peak that gets cut.

ABOUT THE UINTA MOUNTAINS

The Uinta range is one of Utah's mountain treasures, a wonderfully wild area with incredible mountain scenery, abundant animal species, and huge forests. The High Uintas Wilderness Area, which encompasses the core of the range, is a backpacker's paradise with hundreds of miles of roadless land to travel afoot. The range is named after the "Uintat" Indians, a branch of the Ute Tribe who hunted the area. Father Escalante first described the Uintas in 1776, followed by John Wesley Powell in 1869. Many Uinta summits bear the names of early naturalists, surveyors, or explorers: Hayden Peak, Mount Agassiz, Cleveland Peak, Leidy Peak, Marsh Peak, Gilbert Peak, Mount Powell, and Kings Peak (the latter three are 13ers).

The Uinta range is unusual compared to other Rocky Mountain ranges. The most obvious distinction is its orientation, the longest east-west range in the contiguous United States. Also curious (to geologists anyway) is that the range contains none of the igneous rock that is characteristic of the Rocky Mountains, including the Wasatch Range. Instead, the core of the range—the exposed rock forming the peaks—is composed entirely of quartzite of Precambrian age, the oldest rocks in Utah.

Formation of the Range

The Uintas began as ironically as most mountains do, as a wide, deep trough in the earth's crust. Westward-moving streams filled it with thousands of feet of sediment (today's quartzite strata are 20,000 feet thick). Then, along with the rest of the Rockies, massive forces pushed up the area, creating a 150-mile-wide uplift. Over the millennia, multiple weathering processes steadily wore away and sculpted the area. Water erosion cut valleys and created the basic drainage patterns, but glaciers are mainly responsible for the basic look and drama of the range as we see it today. Covering more than 1,000 total square miles of land, glaciers literally dug into the earth, carrying away rock and creating various-sized cirque-headed basins separated by high, rocky, sometimes-precipitous ridges thousands of feet high. The range is the classic Rocky Mountain glaciated landscape, and the largest area of glaciated scenery in Utah.

Dome Peak, view from Island Lake, Henrys Fork basin

The western end of the range was almost completely submerged under an ice sheet created by the merger of several glaciers, and the effects are seen today, with sharper ridges (arêtes and cols) and the most rugged peaks in the Uintas. Not surprisingly, this area includes the 13ers around the East and West Forks of Blacks Fork. As you hike the north-slope trails, or look at topographic-map contour lines, you'll notice the classic U shape created by glaciers, with near-level, gentle drainage bottoms.

In other areas of the Uintas, like the southern slope, broader ridges indicate that glaciers weren't as tightly situated. But the south slope's expansive area housed the largest glaciers in terms of area, so you'll see signs of glaciers everywhere. Some glaciers in the Uinta range reached lengths of 27.5 miles long, more than five times the length of glaciers in the Wasatch Range. On the south slope, glaciers retreated earlier, leaving more erosion time for streams. Thus, you'll often see large V-shaped gorges. The Yellowstone Creek Trail, one less-traveled way to get to Kings Peak, follows one such magnificent gorge.

As the glaciers retreated, powerful "frost-wedging" and other weathering processes began to wear down and crumble the newly exposed bedrock, creating gargantuan piles of talus and boulders. Uinta quartzite, which is fractured yet very hard, is well suited to the production of talus, as every mountaineer can attest.

The Pinnacle on Pinnacle Peak's east face, view into Atwood Basin

Lakes and ponds are another result of glacial activity, and Uinta glaciers were certainly prolific in that regard—on the glaciated portion of the range, topographic maps show more than 4,300 bodies of water larger than fifty feet in diameter. Water bodies are formed when moving ice presses downward, gouging out depressions that later fill with rainwater, or when glaciers deposit material at their edges (known as moraines), forming dams.

One interesting geologic fact is that the Uinta crest used to be the Continental Divide, the northern slopes draining into the Atlantic Ocean. Through a series of complicated geologic events, all the northern streams (as well as streams on the south and east sides of the range, and most of southwestern Wyoming) found their way around the Uinta Mountains, and now drain into the Green River, eventually reaching the Pacific. The western end of the Uintas contains the headwaters of Utah's other major rivers, the Weber, Provo, and Bear.

Flora and Fauna

Hiking almost any Uinta trail into the heart of the range, you'll pass through several elevation zones. As you drive to the trailheads, or hike the first part of some lower trails, you'll pass through sagebrush, juniper, ponderosa, and then aspen. The trails quickly enter into the subalpine zone, at about 9,000 feet, dominated by the vast conifer forests of lodgepole pine intermixed with Douglas fir and blue spruce. Higher up, you'll find Engelmann spruce and subalpine fir. Around the marshes and bogs, flowers to look for are elephant's head, shooting star, and marsh marigold. The showy columbine grows in drier, rocky soils.

The subalpine zone transitions to the alpine zone at around 10,000 to

10,500 feet where the trees thin and meadows become larger and more frequent. The alpine zone starts at timberline (about 11,000 to 11,500 feet), where most climbs to the 13ers begin. This zone is a harsh area for plants and animals. Trees can endure only in stunted clusters, usually in protected spots. You'll find a small selection of grasses, mosses, sedges, and lichens, much of it true alpine tundra that is typical of the northern Rocky Mountain ecosystems.

First Gemini (front) and Mount Emmons (skyline), view from South Kings Peak

This low-lying vegetation includes an assortment of wildflowers that is especially beautiful in early to midsummer. Meadow-growing varieties include the tiny purple-pink alpine laurel and the yellow cinquefoil. In marshy places, elephant's head and yellow-white marsh marigold thrive. Even approaching 13,000 feet near the summits, a variety of wildflowers clings to existence. Cotton grass (which looks like cotton balls) grows in rare high-altitude bogs. In rocky areas, you may see isolated bunches of purple-blue sky pilot or white clusters of Smelowskia calycina, or the more solitary alpine sunflower (called "Old Man of the Mountain").

The Uintas are an important sanctuary for a wide variety of animals. The range hosts nearly five hundred different species, thanks to the great topographical variety—deep forest, marshland, streams and lakes, alpine meadows, rocky ridges—and the huge size of the range. The most commonly seen large mammals are deer, elk, and moose that inhabit the area in summer. But because you'll be climbing above timberline, you also have a good chance of observing a fellow climber, the mountain goat (incidentally, a nonnative animal controversially introduced). Amongst the boulders, the small pika and hoary marmot thrive. Moose are an impressive favorite of most Uinta visitors, and not surprisingly, you can find them around the lakes and rivers of the range. During September, you may even witness some sparring and clashing of bull

Anders Clark, David Rose, and Dennis Clark on the summit of Fortress Peak

moose. Below timberline, typically at the middle elevations or lower, there are quite a few beaver ponds as well as river otter. In the forests, you may see the pine marten or boreal owl. Other birds include the osprey, goshawk, and even the golden eagle. If you're extra lucky, keen-eyed, and light-footed, you may see more elusive and exciting carnivores like cougars, black bears, lynx, wolverines, foxes, mink, or weasels. A little-known fact is that the Uintas used to have grizzly bears as well as wolves—sadly, both were exterminated because of competition with agriculture.

Climate of the Uinta Mountains

Climate can change drastically with altitude. High mountain ranges like the Uintas heavily influence surrounding air masses and thus tend to create their own weather (clouds, precipitation, wind, temperature). Climatically, the Uinta elevations are comparable to the latitudes of central Canada or parts of Alaska—certainly hard to believe when it's hot and sunny at home.

The higher the altitude, the lower the air temperature. The scientific rule is that daytime air masses are about five degrees cooler for every 1,000 feet in elevation gain (in reality, other factors come into play, so it's more like two or three degrees per 1,000 feet). In any case, it's not uncommon for Uinta daytime temperatures to be twenty degrees colder than the surrounding populated

Month	Jan.	Feb.	Mar.	Apr.	May	June	July	Aug.	Sept.	Oct.	Nov.	Dec.
Avg. Max. Temp. (F)	25	27	31	39	48	60	66	65	56	45	30	26
Avg. Min. Temp. (F)	-1	0	6	13	21	28	34	33	26	17	6	0
Sunrise	7:45	7:30	6:55	7:05	6:20	5:50	5:55	6:20	6:50	7:20	6:50	7:25
Sunset	5:05	5:40	6:15	7:45	8:20	8:45	9:00	8:35	7:55	7:05	5:20	4:55
Approx. Light Hrs.	9.5	10	11.5	12.5	14	15	15	14	13	12	10.5	9.5

- **Sunrise/Sunset:** See http://aa.usno.navy.mil for more information. Input used: Lat. 40 deg 47 min N, Long. 110 deg 22 min W for Kings Peak; 7 hrs west of Greenwich; first day of the month. April-October times reflect daylight savings time (+1 hour).
- **Temperatures:** See http://www.wrcc.dri.edu for more information. Data extrapolated to 11,000' elevation, from lower Uinta slope weather station ("Uintalands," 8,400', 1977-1989 data), subtracting -3 degrees per 1,000' gain.
- **Light hours:** Does not include twilight, which may add roughly 1 extra hour.

valleys. Above 11,000 feet, summertime temperatures during the day are rarely above 75 degrees. Nighttime temperatures, even during the warmest months of the year (July and August) can linger near freezing. Lower average temperatures mean that precipitation during hiking season (June, July, August, and September) can vary from rain to hail, sleet, even snow.

The Uintas receive more precipitation in the summer than any other area of Utah. It's not uncommon to reach a summit on a cloudy day only to notice that the clouds are confined to the Uintas, the surrounding land having clear skies. Driving on I-80 into Wyoming, the Uintas are often dishearteningly recognized as the land beneath the huge, dark, precipitating thunderheads. Surprisingly, during the winter months the Uintas get about only *half* the amount of snow as the Wasatch. This fact isn't readily apparent because snowfields actually stick around longer due to lower temperatures.

Protecting the High Uintas

The first protective measures for the Uinta Mountains came from the Forest Service, which designated the 237,000-acre High Uintas Primitive (versus "Wilderness") Area in 1931. Half a century went by before an official wilderness boundary was settled. It happened in 1984 when Congress passed the Utah Wilderness Act, largely a result of Utah Wilderness Association efforts, designating 456,700 acres as the High Uintas Wilderness Area. The act also included eleven other Forest Service wilderness areas statewide.

Although passage of the act was a major success for wilderness, the area protected was actually smaller than what the Utah Wilderness Association had hoped for, having proposed 659,000 acres in 1979. That acreage goal still

First Gemini peak, view from Trail Rider Pass

stands today as the better solution, not just for size, but for its ecologically based focus that preserves entire biological systems.

In order to have truly "wild" experiences, we need truly wild places. However, it's an ideal that is threatened even with wilderness boundaries, artificial lines that don't have any meaning to ecosystems. Top concerns are overgrazing by domestic animals, oil and gas development, and overharvesting of timber— all of which eat away at remaining roadless areas.

One of the unfortunate compromises made to get passage of the United States 1964 Wilderness Act was that grazing of livestock was preserved. In typical Utah style, the state's *own* Wilderness Act went further and handed over ridiculously lenient rights to ranchers on wilderness land. The Uintas currently have forty-three cattle allotments as well as thirty-four sheep allotments, twelve of which (amounting to 13,000 sheep) lie primarily within wilderness boundaries. As a result, it's estimated that more than 60 percent of the Uinta landscape has been badly ecologically damaged. Just think: grizzlies and gray wolves in the Uintas were exterminated to preserve *sheep* ("hoofed locusts," as Edward Abbey put it). Both Forest Service and conservation organizations agree that alpine areas are overgrazed, but disagree as to the solution. Currently, an environmental-impact statement is being prepared for West Fork Blacks Fork, an area of particular concern.

Leasing land for oil and gas development is diminishing roadless areas surrounding the Uintas. U.S. Geological Survey and Forest Service studies estimate that the reserves of fossil fuel under the Uintas would supply the United States with only nine minutes' to two days' worth of oil based on current consumption rates! The Bridger Lake Gas Plant, about three miles from the Henrys Fork Trailhead, has produced only twenty hours' worth of oil in the past thirty years. In spite of this, proposals continually emerge to lease national forest lands for development.

Forest health is another concern. Timber logging disturbs wildlife and fragments natural forests. Interfering with natural processes by managing wildfires and controlling disease is debated. Furthermore, because forests have been overharvested over the decades, most timber cuts are planned for currently roadless areas.

The Wilderness Movement and Guidebooks

The natural tendency of most outdoorsmen upon discovering a beautiful outdoor area is to keep it a secret. For certain specific areas, this could be a valid response. However, generally speaking, and no matter how much we may wish otherwise, increased use of all land is inevitable unless we block access entirely, to everyone, which is clearly an impossible choice.

The question is *who* is using the land, and for *what?* The natural course of industrial mankind is to break down the wilderness into "usable" resources: roads, mines, timber parcels, grazing allotments. The reason we have any protected wildlands at all is due to wilderness champions and supporters—who likely were introduced to these areas by other people. Few of us find out about magnificent areas any other way. I learned about all my favorite backcountry destinations through other people, usually guidebook authors. No matter the method of discovery—articles, organizations, meetings, slide shows—something magical happens when we experience wild places firsthand. The locations change from a pretty photograph or glowing words to something personal and tangible. Those with such experiences are the most likely to become wilderness advocates and defenders. The wilderness movement is, after all, nothing more than a group of people with an active voice. The larger the force, the more protection and wilderness we'll likely have. Hikers' boots pale in comparison to damage done by bulldozers, trucks, and mines. And I'd rather meet up with a hiker in the backcountry any day than the antithesis to the wilderness experience: dirt bikes, ATVs, vehicles, roads, and snowmobiles.

Still, boots and pack animals take a toll, especially in the alpine zones or desert country. Wilderness is shrinking, and the number of backcountry users is mushrooming. Please do your part not only to tread lightly but also to raise a voice for more wilderness status in areas that qualify, before it's too late.

One area currently being pushed for wilderness status in the Uinta Mountains is called the Lakes Backcountry or Mount Watson Wilderness. This large, wild region lies west of the Mirror Lake Highway, and is the largest chunk of roadless area in Utah (more than 100,000 acres), aside from the lands immediately surrounding the wilderness boundary. Find out more about this wilderness proposal by visiting the High Uintas Preservation Council's website at www.hupc.org.

Wilderness Use and Regulations

The High Uintas Wilderness Area is administered by two national forests: the Ashley National Forest (on the south slope) and the Wasatch-Cache National Forest (on the north slope). Refer to the appendix for contact and additional information.

Rough, unscientific usage stats provided by the Forest Service indicate that in 2001 about 12,500 people ventured onto the north-slope trailheads. A whopping one-third of them hiked the Henrys Fork Trail, many of them likely headed for Kings Peak.

In light of this high usage, the Forest Service has issued regulations to protect the area. As pertaining to the hiker (horse packers have additional restrictions), the following are prohibited within the High Uintas Wilderness Area:

- Group size exceeding fourteen persons.
- Camping within two hundred feet of trails, lakes, ponds, springs, and other water sources (terrain permitting).
- Camping within one hundred feet of an occupied campsite.
- Camping for more than fourteen days at an individual site.
- Shortcutting a trail switchback.
- Disposing of debris, garbage, or other waste.

There are also permanent fire closures around some lakes, as you'll read in the trail descriptions.

Interestingly, the rule about not camping within two hundred feet of water wasn't the result of water-pollution issues. Its original purpose was to reduce the "city park" effect of crowded tents surrounding wilderness lakes. However, the rule clearly has the benefit and purpose of reducing water pollution as well.

There are many previously used campsites that are located illegally close to lakeshores and rivers. Scatter out and get away from those high-use lakes whenever possible. Follow the "water rules" (see "Leave No Trace" in the appendix) about depositing all dishwater, human waste, and so on two hundred feet away from water sources.

At present, you do not need a permit to hike or climb in the High Uintas Wilderness Area. However, every year the Forest Service discusses the idea of requiring permits and limiting visitors. It's some years down the road, but they foresee it happening. Permit or no permit, you should register at the trailheads. Doing so allows the Forest Service to gain valuable management data, and provides them with a way to find you if an emergency situation should arise (with you or family at home).

USING THIS GUIDE

Terminology, Symbols, and Clarifications

Shorthand map references like M6.2 or Map 6, P2, for example, mean the point marked as a circled "2" on Map 6. Likewise, M6 means Map 6.

(AN): author's name for peaks or other landforms that don't have official names, to make them easier to reference

ascending traverse or **descending traverse:** angular travel across a mountain slope, climbing or dropping in elevation as you go

cairn: a man-made trail marker consisting of a pile of rocks

cirque: a semicircular, steep-walled, flat-bottomed valley carved by glaciers

CL: an abbreviation for "class" (a route-difficulty rating system)

couloir: a relatively narrow groove cutting through a cliff or rock wall, typically wider than "cracks" and smaller than "gullies"

early season: the first three to four weeks after most snow cover has melted, roughly the last week of June to mid-July

elevation gain: measures the total cumulative vertical elevation gain in feet, including any extra climbing due to up-and-down altitudinal movement, not just the difference between beginning and ending points

elevation loss: same idea as elevation gain, it measures the total cumulative loss in elevation

glissade: a technique used to descend snow slopes by sliding, sitting, or standing, usually controlled by an ice axe

late season: the last four to six weeks of snow-free conditions, roughly the last week of August to mid-October

moraine: mounds of rock debris left by glaciers

mountaineering: the act of climbing mountains; it doesn't have to involve "technical" climbing with ropes or other specialized gear

scree: loose rock, fist-size or smaller, that has fallen from cliffs and ridges

talus: loose rock larger than fist-size, typically large enough to not slide underfoot, that has fallen from cliffs and ridges

technical climbing: any climbing (on rock, ice, or firm snow) that requires the use of ropes and belay anchors for safety or assistance

3-season: the standard meaning is spring, summer, and fall

traverse: horizontal travel across a mountain's face or slopes

2-season: summer and fall, the snow-free hiking and climbing season in the Uintas

Maps

Maps are the foundation of almost any backcountry expedition. I've tried to make the maps in this book more than just a visual support to the route descriptions, but also something you can actually use both in planning and in the field.

Maps 1 and 2 are meant to be general references, but because they were made to scale, you should also find them useful for measurement. Map 2 shows the USGS 7.5" quadrangle topographic-map boundaries. The trail-access maps (Maps 3, 8, 13, and 14) were derived from USGS 1:100,000-scale metric topographic maps. The summit-detail maps (Maps 4–7, 9–12, and 15–18) were derived from USGS 7.5" (1:24,000) topographic quadrangle maps. One great benefit to using these maps in the field is that they often combine more than one 7.5" maps, saving you from having to pack and carry several large, unwieldy maps.

There are two other maps you'll probably need. The first is any basic road map of Utah. But the most important is the High Uintas Wilderness Map (HUWM) produced by the Forest Service, an outstanding map to use while hiking and climbing. The entire wilderness area is contained on one convenient map. It is also topographic (at 200-foot contour-line intervals), highly readable, and more up-to-date than USGS maps. I reference the HUWM trail numbers in the trail descriptions. The HUWM is available at Forest Service district offices and the two supervisor offices that deal with the Uintas, as well as the Utah Natural Resources Map and Bookstore (see the appendix).

Difficulty Ratings

CLASS DIFFICULTY

Class ratings are based on the Yosemite Decimal System (YDS). The YDS describes only the roughest, most "technical" part of the route, no matter the length. That's why I like to throw in class ratings throughout a route description, so the overall rating is put into perspective.

Although the YDS is a standard, most mountainous regions and guidebooks use a customized YDS, and I've done the same thing here. Thus, these ratings won't be directly equal to class ratings for Colorado peaks, for example. Because virtually all Uinta 13er routes fall under two nontechnical classes (2 or 3), I've added a "+" division to be a little more descriptive.

Difficulty ratings and descriptions are for dry conditions in good weather. High winds, wet rocks, and snow cover (new snow or lingering snowfields) can change the rating drastically. And like any difficulty rating, class ratings are subjective. If you want to know how hard a particular route is that I'm calling Class 3, the best way to find out is to try it yourself, and then you'll have a reference point for other climbs.

Class 1: Walking on maintained trails, or off-trail hiking that is just as easy as walking on a trail

Class 1+: Walking on trails of unusual steepness or roughness, or off-trail hiking on stable, consolidated terrain of mild to moderate angle

Class 2: Always off-trail, on a variety of mountainous slopes, including moderate talus/boulder slopes or very steep but consolidated slopes. Class 2 is an average Uinta boulder field or rock slope.

Class 2+: Rougher or steeper rocky slopes where you sometimes use your hands for balance, but you're still mostly using your legs

Class 3: Scrambling (versus walking movements), where you are constantly using your hands for balance or to help upward movement

Class 3+: You must use your upper body muscles to pull upward or drop downward, in simple climbing maneuvers

Class 4: The beginning of easy "technical climbing." You have to search for, select, and test handholds, and your movements are more thoughtful and slower. Beginners may want a rope if the route is long and exposed.

Class 5: Technical rock climbing. You are using a variety of climbing techniques, like stemming, cross-pressure, and the like. This category is broken down into smaller segments, 5.0 to 5.14. Ropes and belays are the standard.

In the descriptions, a class rating in parentheses such as "2+ (4)" means there is a *very short* Class 4 section (for instance, a broken cliff band), but the majority of the climb is Class 2+.

Overall Difficulty

It's not practical to give each 13er an overall difficulty (strenuousness or class) rating. There are multiple trail approaches of varying lengths and difficulties, and if you plan to climb all the 13ers, they are best done in groups and not individually. Even if you assume the easiest or shortest trail and the easiest or shortest route, foregoing any unnecessary peak grouping, the overall rating depends on how the effort is spread out—is it done over several days, or condensed to a high-mileage overnighter? (One-day trips from trailheads aren't realistic for most people.)

The Round-Trip Routes tables for each Group provide a consistent measuring point (base camp) for comparing various routes (peak Groups). Each route in the table has a roman numeral "grade" rating, roughly based on elevation gain and mileage. The final grade I give to a round-trip route is a judgment call, and is relative to all other 13ers, so the route's actual elevation gain and mileage don't have to exactly match the grade definition.

Grade I: Easy. Less than 2,000-foot elevation gain and less than four miles.
Grade II: Moderate. Around 2,500-foot elevation gain and five miles.
Grade III: Strenuous. Around 3,200-foot elevation gain and seven miles.
Grade IV: Very strenuous. Around 4,000-foot elevation gain and ten miles.
Grade V: Extreme. Around 5,000-plus-foot elevation gain and eleven-plus miles.

These grade ratings also closely correspond to the amount of time the route will take. Grade I and II routes will typically take a small part of a day, no more than half a day. Grade IV and V routes will generally take an entire day along with relatively "strenuous" or "extreme" effort.

For individual route segments, the description itself along with the associated stats (class, miles, elevation, and distance) give an accurate picture without adding a subjective word rating.

Time Estimates

The estimates assume *steady hiking with few or no breaks,* in order to keep the estimates fairly consistent. Until you've done a few peaks and know how your pace compares, you should treat the time estimates as rough best-case scenarios, adding additional time for things like lounging around on the summit, lunch, photography, and so on.

Trail time estimates to base-camping areas assume you're carrying a multi-day pack and thus not moving terribly fast. If you're day hiking the trail (or part of it), you will of course go faster. Beyond base-camping areas, day hiking is assumed.

Time estimates are based on my trips, but also happen to closely match an "average" hiking or scrambling pace.

Average Pace Estimates

Hiking with day packs, an average pace for rocky ridges and slopes is 1 to 1.5 mph, and for trails or gentle basin country, 2 mph going up and 3 to 4 mph going down. For backpacking on trails, it's not uncommon to hike in to base camp (with heavier packs) going 1.5 mph or so, and hike out (with lighter packs, downhill) at 3 mph. A good overall backpacking average is 2 mph, adding in a half hour for every 1,000 feet gained in elevation. Whether day hiking or backpacking, going back *down* a route or trail usually takes about two-thirds of the ascending time, except on very rough terrain, where you'll probably end up going the same speed both directions.

Route and Trail Descriptions

Trails and Trailhead Directions

Each of the four main Groups can be accessed by more than one trail, described separately from the route descriptions. The Group introductions discuss the pros and cons of each trail, with specific regard to which trails are ideal for certain peak routes. However, from at least one trail in the Group, you can establish a single base camp and use it to climb every peak in the Group. Driving directions and trailhead descriptions are separate from the Group descriptions to avoid repetition (some Groups use the same access roads).

Primary Routes

Within each Group division, you'll find individual route descriptions organized by peak. These recommended off-trail routes are marked on the maps as a series of solid dots. They are often segments of a larger complete route that includes more than one summit, as indicated in the title (for example, "South Kings Peak, from Kings Peak"). Descents, if different from the ascents, are described as an individual route. Routes are segmented because complete routes sometimes overlap, and there are multiple ways you could combine routes. All routes and peak combos are only suggestions; you'll have to decide if they seem reasonable to you, or if you could actually do more summits in a day (or less summits), or in a different sequence.

It's important to note that all mileage, elevation, and time stats for any given route segment are one-way—and are labeled as such—and refer only to that particular segment. For round-trip summaries of various one-day route combinations, look at the route tables at the beginning of each main Group. They will spare you from having to add the numbers for each segment, and should be a big help in planning your itinerary.

Other Routes

On the summit detail maps, you'll notice routes marked by a series of open dots (circles). *Do not confuse them* with the primary routes described within each Group chapter. Read the appendix for an explanation of these "Other Routes."

Routes in Reverse

The majority of Uinta routes are relatively uncomplicated, mostly just requiring boulder-negotiation skills. Thus, you should be able to do a route opposite to the description direction without problems. There's not much reason to, except that some of the descent routes described in this book would make great ascents. Simply read the description to get an idea of the terrain.

Seasonal Snow and Changing Conditions

It is possible that lingering snowfields of early summer or snowstorms (at any time) may cover some routes, particularly on sunlight-deprived north-facing slopes. Snowfields may disappear in drought years, or become big obstacles after big winters. Trail descriptions were accurate at the time of writing, but trails can degrade or get improved, and cairns and signs may fall or get repaired. Likewise, roads can change overnight after storms.

About Base Camps

All the descriptions and stats are arranged around specific base camps, marked on the maps, mainly to provide a measuring point. But they also have the characteristics of a good base camp: central location to peaks, water sources, scenic value, tent sites, and so on. Most—but not all—are below timberline for better weather protection. You could always camp closer to the summits at higher elevations. If you do camp above well-timbered areas, be aware of the exposure and increased lightning risk. If possible, please avoid the natural tendency to camp in the *exact* spots shown on the maps, which could lead to overused sites. Refer to the appendix for "Leave No Trace" camping techniques, which include the benefits of "dispersed camping."

Route Description Detail

It is impossible to please everyone. Some hikers can get by with or actually prefer vague directives like "hike up the maintained trail and route-find up the west ridge," whereas other hikers like to know every detail. It is a matter of personal opinion. My objective was simply to be as helpful as possible to the average hiker.

Logistics and Itinerary

The focus of this book is doing summit clusters from a base camp, and I see three main strategies to accomplish that objective. The first is a multiday backpack trip with the goal of doing all (or some) of the peaks in one of the four main Groups. The second is a quicker trip that can be done over a full three-day weekend, using the same base-camp areas. The third is a high-mileage overnight trip using a lower campsite (I mention campsite possibilities in the trail descriptions).

Multipeak (Group) Trips

This is the main emphasis of this book, and if you're out to climb all twenty-one summits, it is the most efficient way to do so, as it requires fewer overall days, less energy, less driving, and so on, and because the peaks in each Group are so close together. The first day is spent hiking in to base camp. The next one to four days, or more if desired, are spent climbing the peaks using the routes in this book. The last day you hike out and drive home. The Group trip strategy ensures you make it to all the summits in an unhurried fashion, enjoying the scenery, timing around possible thunderstorms, and even (gasp) doing something else besides climbing peaks. For all-inclusive Group trips, I recommend adding an extra day to your time estimate, to account for bad weather.

Weekend Trips

It's understandable that not everyone has the time or wants to do long trips. Most people can, however, take a weekend trip. If you can swing a full three days, you can complete any of the suggested routes in this book (consisting of one or more 13ers). You'll have an entire day to hike in to a high base camp (the same base camp you would use on an all-inclusive Group trip), a full day to finish a route, and a full day to hike out and drive home.

Overnight Trips

This one is harder, but still doable if you're a strong hiker. Some peaks and peak Groups are close enough that it's not a big deal, but others will take careful planning of miles and time. The idea is to hike in as far as you can the first day, with the understanding that on the second day you'll have to climb the peak(s) from camp, pack up, backpack out, and drive home. Even if you make it all the way to the high base-camping areas, the next day would typically be around fifteen to twenty miles. Such a relatively high-mileage (and high-elevation gain) day is made more possible by three things: most of the miles will be done with light day packs; returning to the trailhead will typically be all downhill; and your overnight pack will be a *little* lighter (depending on how much food you have or haven't eaten!). Those factors also help determine how to divide the miles, that is, how far to hike in the first day. It could be that hiking all the way in to a high base camp is not the best approach. The round-trip summary charts in the introduction to each Group may help you decide. For example, if you hike in eight miles, and the round-trip total is twenty-five miles, then twenty-five less eight gives you a cool seventeen miles to do the next day. Of course, the logistics of this whole idea also depend on what portion of each day you have available.

Single-Day Trips

A few summits are relatively close to the trailhead and aren't difficult to do in a quick overnight or three-day-weekend trip. These same summits are the most likely candidates for one-day hikes, round-trip from the trailhead. This topic is discussed in the appendix.

Longer Trips

It is also logistically easy to include as many 13ers on the same trip as you want (even all of them). The four main Groups I have outlined aren't set in stone. For instance, you could access the majority of the summits by hiking from the north slope to the south slope (or vice versa; see Maps 8, 13, and 14). One great loop hike that connects Groups 2 and 3 uses Henrys Fork, the Lake Hessie Trail (North Slope Highline, not described in this book), Red Castle Trail, and Highline Trail over Anderson Pass (see Map 8). In fact, it would be possible to climb *every* 13er in roughly three weeks. Such a trip would end up being around 125 miles and more than 41,000 feet of total elevation gain.

Enjoy the Summits

With all this strategizing, one thing to consider is that trying to cram every possible peak into a trip is probably not the best way to enjoy them (the boulders can become tiresome after a while). It just depends on your physical ability, time, and personal motivations. You can always come back; hey, it's another excuse to head to the Uintas! Regardless of how many 13ers make it into your schedule, I recommend taking at least one trip longer than a weekend, if possible. You'll undoubtedly find that the longer you're out, the higher the *quality* of your wilderness experience.

When to Go

The timing of your trip can dramatically affect hiking conditions. Factors include precipitation, snow cover, mosquitoes and other biting insects, temperatures, hours in the day, and numbers of other hikers. Keeping in mind that each year can be very different, this section describes typical conditions during the mostly snow-free 2-season hiking period. Refer to the "Climate of the Uinta Mountains" section on page 9 for average monthly temperatures and daylight hours.

June

The Uintas are usually snow-covered until around mid-June or later. It's a time of transition, with large tracts of lingering snow that are melting rapidly in the summer sun and warming daytime temperatures. Mosquitoes are also already hatching quickly.

Early July

By the beginning of July, most trails and passes are open. Larger snowfields will block *some* routes, but you should be able to pick your way around these snowfields and reach the top of any 13er. You can also use snowfields to your advantage on the descent by cautiously glissading. Daytime temperatures average 60–65 degrees; nighttime temperatures linger around the freezing point. Heavy snowmelt turns streams into torrents, sometimes a serious obstacle. Occasionally you can beat the worst of the mosquitoes on an early July trip, but generally mosquitoes will be thick starting even in June. Wildflowers and alpine vegetation in the upper meadows are very beautiful, and scattered snowfields make the mountains more scenic.

Mid-July through August

This is the height of the summer hiking season, a popular time to visit the Uintas. Temperatures in July are the warmest of the year (60–70 degrees), but still considerably cooler and more comfortable than the lower land surrounding the Uinta range. Nighttime temperatures are typically around 30–35 degrees, so you'll still want warm clothing and a warm sleeping bag. Snowfall is of course rare but still possible at such high elevations. Afternoon thunderstorm activity is at the highest, so you'll need to be more cautious about lightning. Stream crossings are moderate. Mosquito populations taper off throughout the summer as the swampy places dry out; by late August there are few mosquitoes left. Temperatures are substantially colder by the end of August.

Late August through September

Fall is a great time to visit the Uintas. Fewer people go during this season, there are no mosquitoes remaining, the fall colors are in full force (starting *early* September), and the weather is invigorating. Very few snow patches remain beyond August; if they do, they're inconspicuous and at the highest elevations. Most (but not all) streams are low enough to hop across on boulders. The weather tends to be better, with longer periods without rain. September is a month of exciting extremes. You can be sweating in sunny, clear weather during a climb, later leaning against a gale-force wind, and finally donning fleece layers as the snow falls at the end of the same day. Precipitation in September is variable; one day it may fall as snow, the next day as a cold rain complete with a lightning storm (however, lightning isn't at its highest danger this time of year). If it does snow, it will usually melt away after the first full day of sunshine. You'll still feel warm in the sun, but as soon as a cloud covers the sun or the wind picks up you'll quickly be chilled. At night the temperature plummets; by late September, it will freeze every night (20–30 degrees). Compared to midsummer, September has about two less hours in the day and sunrise is almost an hour later.

Early to Mid-October

This is the last-minute peak-climbing season (for snow-free conditions). If there is precipitation, you can almost be certain it'll be snow of some form, not rain. Snowfall takes longer to melt, likely sticking around in the shadows and on the north-facing slopes of the peaks. The first *major* snowstorm will put an end to the snow-free peak-climbing season. Snow may melt temporarily on lower trails, but the first huge snowstorm will blanket the higher elevations (the peaks themselves) for good.

Daytime temperatures from the end of September to mid-October are crisp (45–50 degrees), usually cold enough that you'll want to wear a long-sleeve shirt or wind shell all the time, especially on the ridges. Nighttime temperatures are well below freezing (15–20 degrees).

Planning around the Weather

The northeast portion of Utah isn't covered by media forecasts as thoroughly as the Wasatch front, but you can follow Wasatch weather for clues; a bad Wasatch forecast generally means the Uintas will have the same weather (or often worse). You can also check online weather sites, looking at forecasts for towns surrounding the Uintas, namely, Kamas, Evanston, Duchesne,

Roosevelt, or Vernal. See appendix for weather-related websites. Even so, Uinta weather can be quite fickle, and weather forecasting is itself an uncertain science, so all you can do is get a feel for possible weather, and make a decision.

Avoiding the Crowds

The beginning and ending of the hiking season are less crowded. Most people go to the Uintas between mid-July and Labor Day or early September; before and after that time, people tend to stay away, thinking of snow, bugs, or cold.

As for the day of the week to go, it's no surprise that the weekends, particularly holiday weekends, are the most crowded. Sometimes the contrast is dramatic—at popular trailheads like Henrys Fork, where almost everyone starts the climb to Kings Peak, the parking lot could be packed to full capacity by Friday night; by Sunday evening the place will be all but deserted. Christmas Meadows, Henrys Fork, and Red Castle are the most heavily used basins on the north slope. All the other trailheads described in this book are less popular, and crowded parking lots and trails aren't as big an issue.

Hunting Seasons

There is always some big-game hunt going on in the Uinta Mountains from mid-August through November. But only three hunts should have any impact on your plans, and minimal impact at that: moose (various hunts), elk (rifle), and deer (rifle). The moose hunt runs from mid-September (usually the second Saturday) to the end of October. Moose hunters are limited, but some will ride horses deep into the wilderness basins, particularly the broad lake-filled basins with easygoing trails like Henrys Fork. The elk rifle hunt starts the first Saturday in October and runs about two weeks. The Uintas seem to be quite popular for this hunt, clogging certain end-of-road parking (West Fork Blacks Fork is one). The deer rifle hunt runs for nine days, from the third Saturday in October through the next Sunday. It is by far the most popular of any hunt, but by then Uinta snow-free peak climbing is normally over. For the elk and deer rifle hunts, wearing "hunter's orange" is a good idea—at least around the trailheads, as few hunters walk up the trails very far.

PREPARATION, SAFETY, AND TIPS

Clothing, Gear, Cooking, Food, and Water

Hiking to the 13ers isn't, or shouldn't be, complicated. The simplicity of such wilderness trips is part of the attraction. But the wilderness has a way of painfully emphasizing the little details about gear and planning that seem so trivial at home. For exhaustive details on backpacking, read *The Complete Walker,* by Colin Fletcher, or for lightweight backpacking techniques, see Ray Jardine's *Beyond Backpacking.* For advanced mountaineering, study *Mountaineering: The Freedom of the Hills.* This section contains relatively brief but important tips that will help you compile your gear checklist and plan your trip.

Bring clothing and gear suitable for the Uinta climate. In the summer, it rains almost every afternoon. Snow is possible at any time of the year, but more likely in early season or in the fall (though snow from a nonwinter storm typically melts off within a day or so). It's not all "bad" weather, of course. The Uinta Mountains can be devoid of storms for a number of days, very occasionally running into weeks. But conditions can quickly turn nasty. Rain from thunderheads can build within short hours, and storms can arise overnight. A cloud hiding the sun and a sudden wind can instantly lower the "felt" temperature by 30 degrees or more. Finally, remember that the sun's rays are very intense at high altitudes, regardless of air temperature. So climbing a peak in direct summer sun without a breeze can sometimes be hot, sweaty work, but the more important concern is protecting yourself from the sun's radiation by bringing and using sunscreen, lip balm, a hat, and so forth.

CLOTHING

Proper clothing is important for your safety as well as comfort. If at all possible, do not wear cotton clothing (for example, cotton sweatshirts and coats or jeans), as the material dries incredibly slowly and sucks away body heat in the process. Instead, wear clothing made of various synthetic materials (nylon, polypropylene, polyester pile, or fleece, for example). Use the "layering system" consisting of several light, loose-fitting clothing layers—more effective and flexible than one heavy article of clothing. A time-tested three-layer system

26

consists of a next-to-skin synthetic shirt, an insulating fleece jacket, and a windproof-waterproof shell. You can add and subtract layers according to the rapidly changing alpine environment. The shell is perhaps the most important. A Gore-Tex parka, though expensive, can be a lifesaver in cold, wet, windy mountains. Always pack a warm hat, as most body heat is lost through the head. Remember to bring long pants, not just shorts. On late-season (fall) trips, "winterize" your clothing selections appropriately (bring gloves or mittens, a warmer hat, and long underwear). To save energy and move faster on *snow-free* terrain, consider wearing trail running or hiking shoes, instead of the traditional hiking boot.

Gear

An internal frame pack is the all-around best choice, but the "old-style" external frame pack will work just as well for hauling your gear up the trail. For climbing to the summits, take a separate, comfortable day pack large enough to hold the Ten Essentials discussed below. The mummy-style sleeping bag is ideal for backpacking, and in general, a bag with 2 pounds of down or 2.5–3 pounds of synthetic fill will work for the Uinta hiking season. Bring a firm, thin, lightweight insulating ground pad; it is just as important for warmth as your sleeping bag. A reliable 3-season tent is a necessity for protection from inevitable cold Uinta storms and insects; you will never regret bringing one. A closed tent can be ten to fifteen degrees warmer than the outside temperature (an important consideration for freezing fall trips). Make sure it has a working rain fly and can withstand high winds. In selecting your equipment, remember there is no long-term economy or safety in buying or using "cheap," low-quality gear.

Cooking

Campfires are a thing of the past in alpine areas; bring a lightweight, reliable backpacking stove; they're quicker, easier, environmentally friendly, and odor-free, and they allow you to cook anywhere and whenever you want. However, wind will render any stove useless, so bring along a lightweight windscreen. Bring extra fuel; when in doubt, take the extra bottle.

Food

Food is almost as important psychologically as it is physiologically. Bring tasty food you know you'll like. High- and quick-energy foods like dried fruit, candy, candy bars, and nuts and crackers work well for lunch and snacking. Dehydrated foods are best for dinners. To save money over freeze-dried food, simply visit your local grocery store where you'll find plenty of dehydrated foods like rice and pastas that cook quickly (in ten minutes or less). Plan on about 1.5 to 2 pounds of food per person per day, or 3,000 to 4,000 calories, for typical Uinta trekking. Save hassles in camp, and possibly running out of something, by measuring, compacting, and repackaging food before leaving home (especially helpful for longer trips).

Should you bear-proof your food while in the Uintas? Utah is definitely black bear country, but you'd be very lucky to actually see a bear deep in the wilderness. The general rule is, "food-free, litter-free means bear-free," so it follows that the backcountry is safe. I don't know anyone who has taken pre-cautions for bears such as hanging food while in the Uinta wilderness. We can keep it that way by maintaining clean campsites (no dinner scraps or fish guts left lying around). Nonetheless, the Utah Division of Wildlife Resources web-site recommends not keeping food in your tent, probably mostly a precaution for established and popular trailhead campgrounds like Henrys Fork and China Meadows, where bear warnings have been posted. At those trailheads, keep a clean campsite, keep food in your vehicle, and don't ever feed a bear.

A more likely food thief in the Uintas is the "camp robber," the Clark's nut-cracker, a light-gray, medium-size bird that will hang around camp and fly off with almost any food left unattended. Some friends of mine had an entire pack-age of Keebler cookies hauled away, cookie by cookie, by the enterprising birds.

Other potentially bothersome critters include mice, chipmunks, and squir-rels. Backcountry chipmunks and squirrels aren't as bold as those that reside in trailhead campgrounds, but watch them. Mice are the most active at night, and I've often heard them scratching and scrambling over my pack and cookware. Pull draw cords and zip up packs tightly.

Water Access and Treatment

The good news is the Uinta Mountains have abundant water. "Dry" camps within the wilderness area are virtually nonexistent. However, water becomes scarce once you start climbing the boulders to the summits, so you'll need to carry it all in your day pack. The sun can be intense at such high altitudes, so on all-day climbs you may need three quarts or more of water. Depending on the season, you may run across a snowfield, but melted snow water often drops underneath the boulders, making it completely inaccessible. For surface streamlets, a small plastic measuring and dipping cup (the same one you use for cooking) is perfect. If there's still about a half-quart in your water bottle, you could also fill the remainder with snow and let the bottle heat up in an outside pack pocket.

PREPARATION, SAFETY, AND TIPS

Incidentally, the only trailhead described in this book that has tap water is Swift Creek. All trailheads are adjacent to river water, but it's usually not at all convenient. So bring plenty of water in your vehicle for the drive in, camping at the trailhead, the first day's hike, and the drive out.

Any water you obtain from streams and lakes in the Uintas must be treated. *Giardia lamblia* is the main concern and has been found in some Uinta lakes and streams. It's a hard-shelled protozoan that causes extreme bowel distress in humans: diarrhea, bad gas, loss of appetite, abdominal cramps, bloating, as well as fatigue. Symptoms occur one to three weeks after drinking the water. There are several ways to kill *Giardia* bacteria and viruses, according to the latest medical research. (1) Boil your water. All microscopic creatures are killed at 150 degrees, and boiling water at any elevation on earth is well over 150 degrees. This is the sensible way to purify all cooking water since most meals require boiling water anyway. (2) Use chemicals. Iodine (Polar Pure crystals, Potable Aqua tablets, and so on) kills bacteria and viruses, but is less effective in killing *Giardia*. The basic rule is that the longer you let the chemicals work (or the more chemicals you use), the more effective it is. A good strategy is to treat bottles before bed and let the iodine work all night in the relative warmth of your tent. (3) Use water filters or purifiers. If you want tasty water on-demand with no contamination worries, get a lightweight backpacking filter-purifier combo. The drawbacks to these devices are the weight and the fact that pumping does get tiresome, especially as the filter becomes clogged with longer use. It is best to get a model you can clean in the field.

Summit Gear Checklist

The "Ten Essentials" list is a long-standing, commonsense tradition among outdoorsmen. Don't let the familiarity of this list allow you to forget its importance and get careless. Always take these items on day climbs to the peaks. The main purpose of the checklist is preventative (for use throughout an outing), such as having warm clothes to *prevent* hypothermia, using a map *before* you get lost, having enough drinking water to *avoid* dehydration, and so on. However, most items are also in reserve for emergencies and the unexpected, and truly are extra. Just imagine what you might need to survive if stuck overnight on a cold, windy, wet peak. The key word is *extra*. Take more food, water, and clothing than you expect to use (for both summit climbs as well as the overall trip). Don't overdo it, but a few extra high-energy food and cold-weather clothing items can make all the difference.

- extra food
- extra water
- extra clothing
- map
- compass
- flashlight, extra bulb, and extra batteries
- fire-making items
- pocketknife
- personal first-aid kit
- sun protection (sunscreen, sunglasses, lip balm, and hat)

A headlamp is more useful than a handheld flashlight—invaluable for predawn starts, unplanned route-finding after dark, or around camp. Lighters are *much* more reliable than matches, an important benefit for emergencies as well as for everyday tasks like starting stoves and carefully, thoroughly burning toilet paper.

Add to the Ten Essentials any other items you deem important. Perhaps the "Eleventh Essential" for hiking in the Uintas is insect repellent (especially July to mid-August). Some hikers carry an emergency shelter. The most compact, minimalist shelter available is a "space blanket," made of superlightweight, heat-reflective material. A light nylon or Gore-Tex bivouac sack is a heavier option. A small signal mirror is very effective when used on the high summits and ridges. A whistle is one of the best ways to attract help, as your voice won't carry far. Or consider bringing a cell phone—though not for wilderness purists, they can and have saved lives on backcountry trips. From Uinta high points (ridges and peaks), cell phones with long-range adapters can reach the Wasatch front. Multiuse items for any situation include small amounts of fishing line, duct tape, nylon cord, wire, and extra plastic bags.

Mountain Safety Guidelines

About once or twice a year someone is emergency-evacuated (for example, by helicopter) from the Uintas. The majority of reported accidents are "falling accidents" that occur while climbing on boulders, cliffs, or snowfields. Most steep cliff faces are too rotten to climb safely, even with ropes. The majority of your time climbing the 13ers will be spent up on the boulders, sometimes near cliffs. Be very careful. Other commonly reported accidents or emergency situations throughout the years in the Uintas have included high-altitude sickness, being struck by lightning, being thrown from a horse, or getting lost.

In spite of very real mountain hazards, mishaps are the exception rather than the rule. So there's no need to overreact and let fears ruin a trip, but at the same time, by ignoring common sense, weather, and safety guidelines, you're putting yourself at risk. An illness or injury gets much more serious in high and remote mountains. Follow these guidelines:

- Have a healthy respect for the mountains.
- Leave your trip itinerary with a reliable person. A map photocopy with the route highlighted works well.
- Have current advanced first aid training, including CPR.
- Always carry adequate food, proper clothing, and quality equipment.
- Uinta rain is cold and often accompanied by wind, and even Gore-Tex rainwear has its limits, so make camp before you get miserable, or ideally before precipitation starts. Watch for signs of hypothermia in your companions.
- Take precautions for lightning. Refer to the "Lightning and Thunderstorms" section.
- Never let good judgment be overruled by desire when making route or weather decisions, such as making the summit "no matter what."
- Most mishaps take place at the end of the day, at night, or in camp, when you are tired.
- Prepare yourself physically (for your safety as well as enjoyment of the trip).
- Going solo is not recommended, but if you do, being prepared and taking safety precautions are critical.

Hiking Uinta Terrain

Boulder Fields and Rocky Slopes

The ridges above timberline where you'll be climbing are basically huge crumbling heaps of various-size rocks. The size and variety are tremendous: scree and dirt-slide gullies, fields of multiple-ton behemoths, piles of wobbly flat plates, rock fields embedded in soil, and angular rocks recently fallen from cliffs.

It takes a certain amount of balance, agility, and control to hike and scramble the boulders, and it's the hardest part about climbing in the Uintas. However, the main "technique" is really all about safety and paying attention.

Uinta boulders are potentially rather hazardous—*potentially* hazardous because mis-haps are usually the hiker's fault. Most boulder fields and slopes will require your undivided attention and focus, and it is easy to get distracted by conversation or looking around. Not all slopes are so demanding (easier vegetated segments are common), and the routes in this book avoid any perilous slopes. But you will encounter rocking, wobbly boulders at some point on all routes, unfortunately making a sprain or other injury possible. You must quickly assess every boulder, ready to move nimbly to the next one (the "boulder dance"). Be particularly careful of stepping up onto boulders that can shift down onto your foot or leg. Descending or traversing requires the most control. Also, when climbing up or down loose slopes with a group of people, avoid hiking in a line; instead, spread out a little—even small rocks kicked loose quickly gain deadly momentum. And walk quickly across rock-slide paths, just in case.

Keep it all in perspective, though—the boulder fields are overall quite stable, and the rocks have had thousands of years to settle into place. The bottom line is that climbing on Uinta boulders is generally safe (even fun sometimes) *if* you take the commonsense precaution to watch your step.

Stream Crossings

Always go prepared to wade cold, swift streams. Bridges and makeshift log crossings can wash or rot away, and water levels vary from season to season. Bring a separate pair of wading shoes. Also consider finding a sturdy stick or hiking pole for tough crossings. It is an invaluable balancing aid, as most Uinta streambeds are composed entirely of rounded, treacherously slippery rocks. It is also very easy to underestimate the force of water. When crossing a strong current, face upstream, stabbing a pole upstream for a third point. Early summer (June and July) streams can be particularly problematic. If a stream makes you uneasy, see what it looks like in the morning when water levels are lowest. Late August or September has the lowest water of the hiking season, often allowing you to easily wade or boulder-hop across the same streams that were torrential in July.

Amy Rose wades the chilly West Fork Blacks Fork in September

Ray Overson descends Pyramid Peak's east ridge

CROSSING SNOWFIELDS

If a snowfield has been heated and softened by the sun, and isn't too steep, you can often cross in plain old shoes. Otherwise, you'll want hard-soled boots to get an edge, or safety equipment such as an ice axe or rope or both, especially on hard-frozen snow or really steep and long snowfields. Also be careful getting on and off snowfields—the edges melt faster, so you can plunge down into the gaps between boulders. On descent, the snow glissade is one of the more enjoyable and certainly faster ways to go down. If you're skilled with an ice axe, you could purposefully plan on some nice, long glissades by going a bit earlier than the standard hiking season, perhaps mid-June. Just use your best judgment, and don't attempt snowfields that you are at all unsure about.

CLIFFS

Some routes require you to go around or underneath cliffs. Sometimes the best technique for climbing around a cliff band is at the very base, touching or within arm's length of the cliff band, where the boulders are usually the most stable and the cliff face itself can provide something to balance from. However, the Uintas are an old, crumbling range, and unlike boulder fields that have more-or-less settled into place, the cliffs have rockfall dangers. Eye the rocks above suspiciously, and don't hang out under rock faces or in slide paths, especially crumbly looking ones.

Hiking Techniques

As you ascend to the summits, a few simple hiking and climbing techniques can make a big difference in your energy. For instance, particularly on steep slopes and if you're tired, you can essentially lessen the slope angle by making your own "switchbacks" (zigzagging upwards). Also, getting into some kind of breathing and stepping rhythm helps. If you're struggling with the altitude, use the "rest-step" technique: before the next step up, rest for a moment on your rear leg, with locked knee, and take in a deep breath or two. Another tip is to take regular, short, sit-down rests. In the first five to seven minutes of muscular rest, your body gets rid of a full one-third of the lactic-acid buildup, which is the cause of muscle soreness.

Navigation

Generally speaking, it would be difficult to get hopelessly lost while climbing the 13ers. Established trails lead to the route takeoff points, and all but two of the primary routes described in this book start near timberline. Once you're above timberline, all routes have wide-open views. Nevertheless, it is assumed that you have at least rudimentary topographic map–reading skills—enough to figure out your approximate location, where the summits are, which general direction to go, and if you are still on route. Follow your location on topographic maps as you hike or climb. If you're a competent map reader and trail follower, the truth is you probably won't need a compass to climb the 13ers. However, for personal safety, always bring a full-version orienteering compass and know how to use it (magnetic-declination adjustments, triangulation, and the like). One oft-overlooked navigational aid, particularly for heavily forested areas with limited views, is your humble watch, used in combination with your estimated pace.

Route-Finding

The goal is to pick a path to and from the summits that is safe and within the limitations of your climbing group. Because the 13ers are nontechnical, this requires common sense and boulder-hopping ability more than anything. Even so, "common sense" is relative and requires a certain degree of skill that comes from experience. On certain routes, the specific line you take (even if just yards or feet away from another line of travel) can make all the difference, sometimes turning a Class 3 into a Class 4, or a Class 4 into a rock climb. Most route-finding happens as you climb, making wise decisions from moment to moment, but you can use topographic-map contour lines ahead of time to estimate slope angles or help plan alternative routes. It's easy to miss key obstacles and suddenly not have any view but the slope in front of you. As you hike in from the trailhead, and as you approach the base of a peak, take mental notes of slope angles and the locations of cliff bands and snowfields, and come up with your own route plan.

Lightning and Thunderstorms

Most summer rain in the Uintas (like the Rockies in general) happens in the form of thunderstorms, which carry with them potentially dangerous lightning. Thunderstorms typically develop in the afternoon. They can sneak up on you because they often start out as the fair-weather, compact, puffy white cumulus clouds you'll see scattered about the sky. These clouds are formed as the sun heats a mountain's slopes. When enough vertical convection currents and moisture are present, they start to tower up (sometimes reaching up to an amazing eleven miles high) and build into the thick cumulonimbus clouds with dark bases. When a cumulonimbus cloud reaches the highest levels, its top sometimes flattens and spreads out, the entire formation resembling an anvil. These anvil-shaped cumulonimbus clouds will most assuredly bring precipitation and lightning if they pass or build overhead. This prediction pattern isn't an exact science, of course—cumulus clouds don't always build into cumulonimbus, and sometimes cumulonimbus clouds can become quite large and never turn into a thunderstorm. But generally, when the towering process begins, you can expect rain and lightning.

LIGHTNING FACTS

Lightning is Utah's number-one weather-related killer, and is the greatest external hazard to summer peak climbing in the Uintas. On average, lightning kills one person per year in Utah, and every other year or so someone is struck in the Uinta Mountains. Although lightning "season" throughout the United States is April through October—covering the entire snow-free climbing season in the Uintas—the majority of lightning strikes, injuries, and deaths happen in June, July, and August, with July being the most deadly. As a peak climber, you have increased risk. Taking the ratio of lightning accidents to population, Rocky Mountain states are near the top of statistical charts (Utah is fifteenth on one list). Analytically, chance is on your side (perhaps driving a car is more dangerous, and for comparison, snow avalanches account for four deaths per year in Utah), but lightning is nothing to be trifled with. Direct hits in remote mountains are usually fatal.

LIGHTNING SAFETY

The cardinal rule for lightning safety—and the one that is the most difficult to abide by while climbing in the Uintas—is this: *Do not be the tallest object in your immediate vicinity.* A natural second rule is: *Do not be immediately next to the tallest object.* More than anything else, lightning is attracted to height. What you're holding, packing, or sitting on is unimportant by comparison. Secondary discharges can jump to nearby objects up to ten feet away (stay away from bases of trees).

On Uinta summit climbs, you are typically on exposed ridges or in wide-open areas above timberline. It can take a long time to hike to the point where you are not the tallest object around, so it's critical to plan ahead. As you hike, constantly assess the current risk: How fast are clouds building or nearby storms developing and moving? What is your exposure—how long will it take you to descend or move to safer areas? Be prepared to abandon your plans. Start your ascent early to avoid the typical lightning cycle, and, if possible, be back in the basin by early afternoon.

Warning Signals and Guidelines
- Count the seconds between flash and thunder, and then divide by five to calculate the distance in miles. Repeat to determine if lightning is approaching,
- Follow the thirty-thirty guideline. If flash-to-bang times are thirty seconds or less, take immediate safety precautions. Maintain these precautions for thirty minutes after the storm has passed (the most lightning deaths or injuries occur *after* the most intense rain and lightning).
- Precipitation from a thunderhead, even if it is seen but not felt, is a big warning flag since lightning often begins at the same time as rain.

If You Are Caught in a Storm above Timberline
- Remember, you cannot outrun a storm. Spread out the group so if someone is hit, those unaffected can give assistance. Drop your pack and any metal objects. Squat down, ideally on insulating material like moss, vegetation, snow, or dirt (boulders or rocks are okay but not ideal), keeping your feet together and your head low. Put your elbows on your knees and your hands on your head, so if you are struck, the electrical current will skip the longer path through the vital organs. To avoid deadly ground currents from a nearby strike, don't shelter under an overhang or rock, avoid wet surface cracks, do not lie down, and do not lean against or touch rocks that are to the side of you.

PREPARATION, SAFETY, AND TIPS

- If someone is struck, immediately administer CPR to restore breathing. Electrical burns can be life-threatening; treat them as any other burn.

Hypothermia

Hypothermia—the lowering of the body's inner core temperature when heat loss is greater than heat gain—is the number-one cause of death for outdoorsmen. Surprisingly, most hypothermia cases develop in air temperatures between thirty and fifty degrees, *not* in bitter subfreezing temperatures. Even on a sunny day, a careless outdoorsman can lose great amounts of heat, increasing the risk of developing hypothermia.

The stages of hypothermia, in order of progression, are: uncontrollable shivering, fumbling hands, difficulty speaking, forgetfulness, stumbling, stiff muscles, an inability to get up after resting, irrationality, disorientation, stupor, a weak pulse, blue skin, drowsiness, unconsciousness, and finally death.

The most important thing is to recognize the advance warning signals your body gives you—specifically, *shivering* or feeling the need to exercise to keep warm. Immediately put on a warm hat and warmer clothing (always be prepared!), and consume instant-energy sweets and carbohydrates. Windchill and getting wet are a particularly nefarious combination; seek shelter or put on a protective outer shell.

Never ignore uncontrollable, near-violent shivering. It means "real" hypothermia (versus its warning signals) has set in, and requires drastic action. It is important to realize that hypothermia deprives you of judgment and reasoning power. *You do not realize that it is happening, and you become unable to recognize your own condition.* In addition, loss of hand control makes self-treatment nearly impossible. A person experiencing hypothermia may deny it, claiming everything is fine. Believe the evidence, not the person.

Assist mildly impaired victims into the best shelter available, out of wet clothing and into dry garments, and inside a sleeping bag (prewarmed by another person, because a hypothermia victim's body cannot produce the heat needed to warm both the bag and himself). For the most serious cases, put the victim stripped into a sleeping bag with another person also stripped, maintaining body-to-body contact.

High-Altitude Miseries and Concerns

Decreased oxygen at high altitudes can cause a number of ailments that range from merely uncomfortable to potentially fatal; all ailments fall under "altitude sicknesses." The body is actually quite capable of handling high altitudes—sickness generally occurs only when you go too high, too fast, so your body cannot adjust ("acclimatize"). If you take quick weekenders or otherwise ascend rapidly to the summits, you are more vulnerable. However, it can affect anyone, regardless of age, gender, or physical conditioning. In fact, around 75 percent of hikers going above 10,000 feet will feel some kind of symptoms, most commonly acute mountain sickness (AMS). Climbing the 13ers, you'll start at 8,000 to 9,000 feet at the trailhead and spend most of your time above 11,000 feet, the average elevation for base-camp areas. People coming from near sea level will have a harder adjustment than most residents of Utah or surrounding states, who are somewhat more acclimatized (most towns in Utah are about 4,000–6,000 feet in elevation).

Typical first symptoms of AMS include a loss of appetite and a headache. Later, you may have nausea and insomnia, feel weak or dizzy, and be short of breath. For mild cases, it's safe to continue in moderation, and symptoms usually diminish within three days. If symptoms worsen into vomiting, a splitting headache, and disabling weakness, you should descend to lower elevations.

To treat mild AMS (or avoid it altogether), ascend gradually, taking frequent rest stops. Strenuous exertion makes matters worse. Consider deep breathing (hyperventilation). In quick ascents to high altitudes, the body is laboring intensely to supply oxygen, so avoid large meals or food loaded in fats or proteins that demand more of the body's resources. Instead, eat simple sugars like candy and carbohydrates frequently and lightly. Only trial and error can reveal what food a person's body can tolerate at higher altitudes. Ibuprofen works wonders on headaches, and for any altitude sickness, even a descent of several hundred feet can make a big difference.

High-altitude diseases such as high-altitude pulmonary edema (HAPE) and high-altitude cerebral edema (HACE) are possible but unlikely to happen while you're climbing in the Uintas. The average elevation where these diseases occur is 12,000 feet in the United States. If AMS-like symptoms evolve into noisy breathing (particularly at night), chest pain, coughing up or spitting blood (HAPE), or disorientation, memory loss, hallucination, or psychotic behavior (HACE), descend to lower elevations immediately.

DRIVING TO THE TRAILHEADS

The roads described in this book are generally well signed and maintained. Most roads get rough only near the trailheads. You could drive a passenger car to all the trailheads, but a four-wheel-drive vehicle is generally recommended for any Uinta mountain dirt roads. The West Fork Blacks Fork Road (the last 4.8 miles to the Car Park) deserves special mention. I have driven my passenger car on the road several times—to the Car Park (see Maps 2 and 3), not beyond the river crossing—but it is very rough, and a four-wheel-drive vehicle is advised.

Although your drive in should be straightforward, detailed road logs are provided to reassure and to keep you apprised of what lies ahead, including junctions and campground locations. Few things are more exasperating than wasting any hiking time driving around trying to find the trailhead or a place to camp. Also, due to the vastness of the Uinta Mountains, it's hard to find a good, detailed map that covers the entire distance from highway to trailhead.

Use the Trailhead Access map (Map 1) for a clear overview of all the required roads and highways, then use the road logs for the details. The mph figures indicate the relative roughness of the road (not speed limit signs), so the lower the mph figure, the rougher the road is and the longer it'll take to drive.

Trailhead descriptions are included with the road logs. Read them for important parking and camping information.

North Slope Trailheads from I-80

You can drive to any of the north slope trailheads—Henrys Fork, China Meadows, West Fork Blacks Fork, and East Fork Blacks Fork—starting from the same place: I-80's Exit 34 in Wyoming (the "Fort Bridger" Business I-80–loop exit). Directions for these roads are broken up into seven linked branches, all originating from Exit 34. When you reach an *Important Junction,* simply jump to the next appropriate branch as indicated. Mileage is cumulative from I-80 Exit 34 to the trailheads (it doesn't start over at each segment).

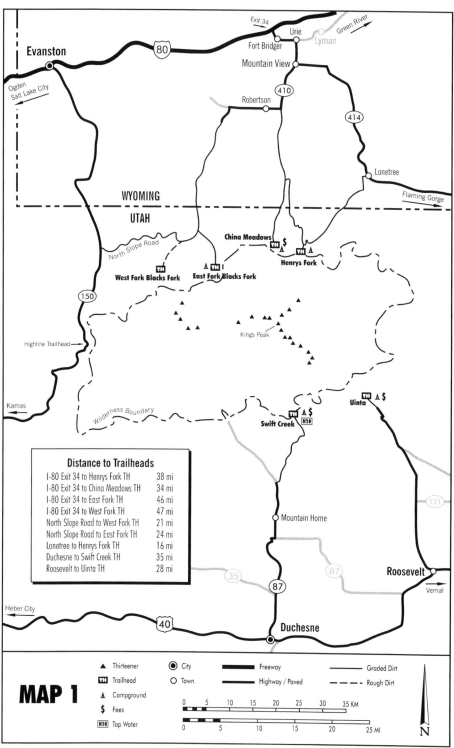

Evanston

80

Exit 34
Urie
Fort Bridger
Lyman   Green River
Mountain View

Ogden
Salt Lake City

410

Robertson

414

Lonetree

Flaming Gorge

WYOMING
UTAH

North Slope Road

China Meadows ▲ $
▲ TH ▲
Henrys Fork

150

West Fork Blacks Fork TH

East Fork Blacks Fork
▲ TH I

▲
▲ ▲ ▲
▲
▲ ▲ ▲
Kings Peak
▲ ▲
▲
▲

Highline Trailhead →

Kamas

Wilderness Boundary

TH ▲ $
Uinta

TH ▲ $
H2O
Swift Creek

Distance to Trailheads

I-80 Exit 34 to Henrys Fork TH	38 mi
I-80 Exit 34 to China Meadows TH	34 mi
I-80 Exit 34 to East Fork TH	46 mi
I-80 Exit 34 to West Fork TH	47 mi
North Slope Road to West Fork TH	21 mi
North Slope Road to East Fork TH	24 mi
Lonetree to Henrys Fork TH	16 mi
Duchesne to Swift Creek TH	35 mi
Roosevelt to Uinta TH	28 mi

Mountain Home

121

35   87

Roosevelt

Vernal

Heber City ←

40

87

Duchesne

MAP 1

▲ Thirteener	◉ City	▬▬ Freeway	─── Graded Dirt
TH Trailhead	○ Town	── Highway / Paved	- - - Rough Dirt
▲ Campground			
$ Fees			
H2O Tap Water			

0   5   10   15   20   25   30   35 KM

0   5   10   15   20   25 MI

N

Trailhead Access

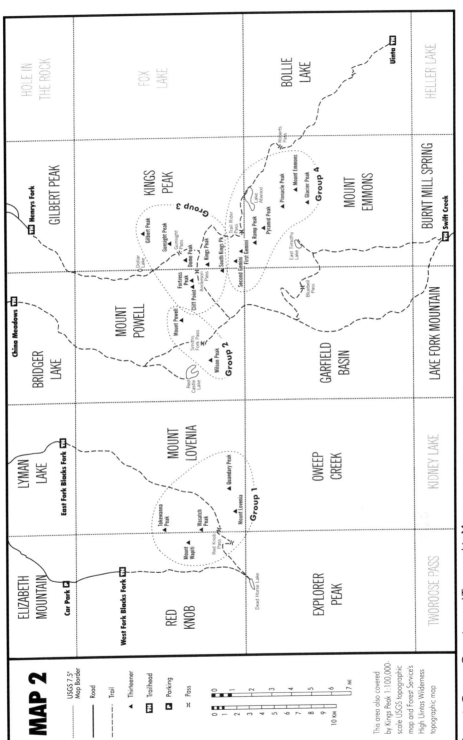

Summit Groups Overview and Topographic Maps

Estimated Driving Times:
> Salt Lake City to Exit 34 on I-80: 2 hours
> From I-80 Exit 34 to:
>> Henrys Fork Trailhead: 1 hour, 15 minutes
>> China Meadows Trailhead (East Fork Smiths Fork Trail): 1 hour, 15 minutes
>> West Fork Blacks Fork Trailhead: 2 hours, 15 minutes
>> East Fork Blacks Fork Trailhead: 1 hour, 45 minutes

BRANCH 1 (STARTING POINT)

0.0   Exit 34. After exiting, turn right, following signs to Fort Bridger.

2.1   Fort Bridger. The highway curves left out of town, passing by a minor paved road (at 2.7) to the right.

5.1   Urie. At the four-way stop and blinking light, turn right (south) on Wyoming Highway 414 toward Mountain View.

7.4   Mountain View. Groceries, restaurants, gasoline.

8.3   Y junction in Mountain View. Turn right on Wyoming 410 toward Robertson (the road to the left goes to Lonetree, Wyoming).

9.3   Pass by a minor paved road (Wyoming Highway 411).

15.2   *Important Junction*

> • STRAIGHT on a dirt road: China Meadows and Henrys Fork Trailhead. A sign points ahead to Wasatch National Forest. 40–50 mph. *Go to Branch 2.*
> • RIGHT (a sharp ninety-degree curve, still on highway): West Fork Blacks Fork and East Fork Blacks Fork Trailheads via town of Robertson. *Go to Branch 3.*

BRANCH 2 (CONTINUING FROM BRANCH 1)
To China Meadows Trailhead or Henrys Fork Trailhead

22.3   Junction. Continue STRAIGHT, following signs to China Meadows and Stateline Dam (the other road goes to Gilbert Meadows).

26.1   Minor junction. Continue STRAIGHT (the road coming in from the right goes to a so-called Deadhorse Trailhead).

27.0   *Important Junction*

> • LEFT: Henrys Fork Trailhead. 30–40 mph. *Go to Branch 4.*
> • STRAIGHT: China Meadows Trailhead. 30–40 mph. *Go to Branch 5.*

BRANCH 3 (Continuing from Branch 1)
To East Fork Blacks Fork or West Fork Blacks Fork Trailheads

17.4   Robertson.
21.6   Junction. Turn LEFT onto a paved road (Uinta County Road 271), leaving the main highway. Signs point left to Blacks Fork Access Area and Meeks Cabin. 55 mph.
23.2   Pavement and winter maintenance end. 40–50 mph.
34.4   Pass by Meeks Cabin Dam side road. 25–35 mph.
36.6   Pass by Meeks Cabin Campground. 15–25 mph.
39.4   Junction. Continue STRAIGHT (road to left goes to Hewinta Guard Station).
40.0   *Important Junction*

   • RIGHT: West Fork Blacks Fork Trailhead and Lyman Lake. Rough, 10–15 mph, sometimes narrow for two cars. *Go to Branch 6.*
   • STRAIGHT: East Fork Blacks Fork Trail. 10–15 mph, rougher. *Go to Branch 7.*

BRANCH 4 (Continuing from Branch 2)
To Henrys Fork Trailhead

28.7   Prominent side road coming in from back left.
29.3   Pass by side road to Whiskey Springs coming in from the left.
29.4   Pass by side road to Graham Reservoir coming in from the right.
30.9   Pass by side road to Table Mountain–Louse Creek coming in from the left. You'll immediately start a winding descent with two sharp switchbacks.
31.9   Dahlgreen Creek. Much-used car-camping areas on both sides of road. Couple of sharp curves going uphill. Next two miles you'll pass by several minor side service roads.
34.1   Junction: Continue STRAIGHT to reach Henrys Fork Trailhead. 15-20 mph. *Note:* The left-hand road comes from Lonetree, Wyoming, an alternative access to Henrys Fork. See page 46 for directions coming in.

36.9   Y junction. Continue STRAIGHT (Hole in the Rock road goes left). 10–15 mph.
37.2   TRAILHEAD 1 and parking area, mainly used by horse packers.
37.5   TRAILHEAD 2, hiker's trailhead.

Henrys Fork Trailhead: No fees are currently being charged for parking or camping at this trailhead. There is no tap water available at either trailhead (untreated water is piped to the horse trailhead), but the river is close by. The horse trailhead has pit toilets, one picnic table, and one camping spot. The hikers' trailhead parking lot and campground is small considering its popularity. It has pit toilets, four picnic tables with campsites, and a couple of nonofficial sites. On crowded weekends the upper parking lot can be full. If the campground is full, you can camp by the roadside. There are several large roadside camping areas between the Lonetree junction (mile 34.1) and the Hole in the Rock junction (mile 36.9), and a nice roadside camping area midway between the two trailheads. See "Henrys Fork Trail" description on page 98 and Map 8.

BRANCH 5 (CONTINUING FROM BRANCH 2)
To China Meadows Trailhead

29.5   Pass by Stateline Dam road.
29.6   Paved surface begins, ends in one-third mile at Stateline Campground entrance.
30.5   Pass by Bridger Lake Campground entrance.
32.1   Pass by East Marsh Lake Campground entrance. West Marsh Lake Campground is at mile 32.2.
33.5   Bridge over East Fork Smiths Fork. Now entering the meadows of China Meadows.
33.7   Major junction. Turn LEFT, following the signs to China Meadows Campground and Trailhead Campground. 15-25 mph.
33.8   China Meadows Campground.
34.3   Trailhead campground entrance. Turn RIGHT to reach the TRAILHEAD at mile 34.4.

China Meadows Trailhead: Both the China Meadows Campground and the Trailhead Campground charge a fee for overnight camping. Also, some years the Forest Service has charged a small fee for parking at the trailhead, at the time of this writing good for about five consecutive days. There are also plenty of existing roadside campsites you could use. The China Meadows Campground has nine campsites with tables, no tap water, and a pit toilet. Some sites are near the shore of a small lake. The Trailhead Campground has pit toilets and fourteen sites with tables, no tap water, and the river isn't close enough for convenient use. Horse packers conglomerate around the sites farthest from the trailhead. The trailhead itself has a large billboard with the typical information about wildlife, wilderness regulations, simple maps, and the like, and even a picnic table. See "East Fork Smiths Fork Trail" description on page 82 and Map 8.

BRANCH 6 (CONTINUING FROM BRANCH 3)
To West Fork Blacks Fork Trailhead

42.4   Junction(2.4 miles from East Fork Blacks Fork junction at mile 40.0). Continue STRAIGHT to reach the West Fork Blacks Fork Trailhead. The road goes west for a short distance, and then curves south. 5–10 mph, very rough, four-wheel-drive vehicle best. *Note:* The right-hand road is the North Slope Road from Highway 150, am alternative access to the Blacks Fork trailheads. See page 47 for directions coming in.
42.7   Pass by a minor side road on left that crosses river on bridge.
46.7   Cross a small stream.
47.2   CAR PARK at a major river crossing.

West Fork Car Park: Beyond the river crossing, a primitive road continues for another three and one-half miles before reaching the beginning of the hiking trail. However, it is recommended that you park here and walk the primitive road (included in the "West Fork Blacks Fork Trail" description). With soft sand and gravel, this river crossing is risky even for four-wheel-drive vehicles, and the road gets much rougher and has seen plenty of damage and abuse from vehicles. Also, the Forest Service's High Uintas Wilderness Map shows this river crossing as the trailhead. There is a sizable flat area for parking at the river's edge, or, if the road is too rough to get that far, there are plenty of places you can pull off the road earlier. There are several well-used car-camping pullouts after the small stream at mile 46.7, but no official campground or any amenities. See "West Fork Blacks Fork Trail" description on page 55 and Map 3.

BRANCH 7 (CONTINUING FROM BRANCH 3)
To East Fork Blacks Fork Trailhead

40.6   Cross bridge over West Fork Blacks Fork River.
45.1   Cross Bear River Smiths Fork Trail.
45.8   TRAILHEAD and camping area.

East Fork Trailhead: A large bulletin board located at the top of an uphill curve marks the entrance to the camping area, as well as the start of the trail. After the board, the road splits: turn right, then left, into the gravel parking lot. The campground has seven campsites, plenty of other flat tent spots, about six picnic tables, and pit toilets, but no tap water. The river is a short walk away. There are no fees at this time, but this could change in the future, as added services are a possibility for the area. The East Fork Blacks Fork Guard Station is about one-half mile up the road from the campground. See "East Fork Blacks Fork Trail" description on page 58 and Map 3.

Henrys Fork Trailhead from Lonetree

This route to Henrys Fork Trailhead is an all-dirt road that branches off Highway 414 near the tiny town of Lonetree, Wyoming. The junction is easy to miss: there isn't a sign marking the turnoff, and Lonetree itself isn't obvious because there aren't many houses visible from the road. If you're coming from the north, you'll see the only Lonetree sign at milepost 121, followed by the turnoff immediately after milepost 122. If you're coming from the south, you'll see signs to Hole in the Rock and Hoop Lake around milepost 123, and the turnoff immediately before milepost 122. Once you turn off onto the dirt road, you'll see signs verifying your route to Henrys Fork.

Estimated Driving Time: 25 minutes

0.0	Leave Wyoming Highway 414, onto dirt road (Uinta County Road 290). 45–50 mph.
0.9	Junction. Turn LEFT onto Uinta County Road 291. A sign also points left to Henrys Fork and Hoop Lake.
2.2	Junction. Turn sharp RIGHT. A sign points right to Henrys Fork (Hoop Lake road goes straight). 20–30 mph.
2.6	Prominent Y junction. Go RIGHT.
7.1	Minor Y junction. Veer RIGHT. A couple more minor roads enter next two miles. Stay straight on the main road.
8.8	National Forest boundary. Better road, 30–40 mph.
9.8	Junction. Continue STRAIGHT (the rougher Hole in the Rock road goes left). A couple of minor side service roads next one and a half miles. Stay straight on the main road.
11.5	Picnic area by Bridger Lake Gas Plant (with informational sign). Road crosses river and passes the gas plant service road on the other side.
11.7	Quarter Corner Trailhead. Continue STRAIGHT.
12.3	Junction. Turn LEFT to reach the Henrys Fork Trailhead and Campground. *Note:* The right-hand road comes from Mountain View and I-80 in Wyoming, an alternative access to Henrys Fork. The road turns

right and goes uphill. See description on page 39 for directions coming in.

15.1   Y junction. Continue STRAIGHT (Hole in the Rock road goes left). 10–15 mph.

15.4   TRAILHEAD 1, and parking area, mainly used by horse packers.

15.7   TRAILHEAD 2, hiker's trailhead. See page 44 for Henrys Fork Trailhead description.

Blacks Fork Trailheads via North Slope Road

Using the North Slope Road, you can reach both the West Fork Blacks Fork Trailhead and the East Fork Blacks Fork Trailhead. From Salt Lake City and vicinity, it is faster than the I-80 approach, but it can be rougher. The entire road is graded dirt, and likely suitable for most cars, but some sections get quite rocky. The road leaves Utah's Highway 150 (Mirror Lake Highway) about 29 miles south of Evanston, Wyoming, and 49 miles northeast of Kamas, Utah. From Kamas, drive on Highway 150 over Bald Mountain Pass (the high point) and past Mirror Lake. Drive 14.7 miles past the Highline Trailhead and turn east (right) at the signs pointing to East Fork Boy Scout Camp and Blacks Fork River. As you drive east on the North Slope Road, you'll pass by many minor side roads. The following mileages are cumulative, ending at one of the Blacks Fork trailheads.

Estimated Driving Times:

From Salt Lake City to the North Slope Road junction on Highway 150: 1 hour, 30 minutes

Highway 150–North Slope Road junction to:

West Fork Trailhead: 1 hour, 45 minutes

East Fork Trailhead: 1 hour, 30 minutes

0.0   Leave Highway 150 (Mirror Lake Highway). 20–25 mph.

1.6   Junction. Continue STRAIGHT (East Fork Bear River Boy Scout Camp road goes right).

2.4   Junction. Continue STRAIGHT (a prominent road goes left).

3.8   Pass by side road to Carter Creek Camp.

4.4   Pass by minor road on right.

6.1   Junction. Continue STRAIGHT (Mill Creek Road 349 goes right).

6.4   Pass by another Mill Creek Road to right.

11.1   Elizabeth Ridge pass (highest point of North Slope Road). Now rougher, 10–15 mph.

16.0   Junction. Turn RIGHT (a road to Lyman Lake road goes straight).

Important Junction (about 100 feet from previous)

• RIGHT: The road to West Fork Trailhead. It goes due west (the opposite way you've been traveling) for a short distance, then curves south for the rest of the way. 5-10 mph, very rough, four-wheel-drive vehicle best.

• LEFT: The road to East Fork Trailhead. 10-15 mph, rougher, sometimes narrow for two cars.

TO EAST FORK BLACKS FORK TRAILHEAD

18.4   Junction (2.4 miles from previous junction at mile 16.0). Turn RIGHT to reach East Fork Blacks Fork trailhead. 10–15 mph. *Note:* The left-hand road comes from Robertson, Wyoming, and I-80, an alternative access to the Blacks Fork trailheads. See page 39 for directions coming in.

19.0   Cross bridge over West Fork Blacks Fork River.

23.5   Cross Bear River Smiths Fork Trail.

24.2   TRAILHEAD and camping area. For trailhead description, see Branch 7 in I-80 access section on page 45.

TO WEST FORK BLACKS FORK TRAILHEAD

16.3   Pass by minor side road on left that crosses river on bridge.

20.3   Cross a small stream.

20.8   CAR PARK at a major river crossing. For trailhead description, see Branch 6 in I-80 access section on page 45.

Swift Creek Trailhead

This trailhead is the starting point for both the Swift Creek Trail and the Yellowstone Creek Trail. Take Highway 40 to downtown Duchesne. You'll see signs (to Yellowstone Canyon, Moon Lake, and Upper Stillwater Reservoir) pointing north onto Highway 87.

Estimated Driving Times:
    Salt Lake City to Duchesne: 2 hours
    Duchesne to the trailhead: 1 hour

0.0   Duchesne. Last chance for gasoline. Turn LEFT (north) onto Highway 87.

5.8   Junction. Continue STRAIGHT (a paved road goes left to Tabiona on State Highway 35).

13.1　Pass by a minor paved road going left to Talmadge.

14.8　Bottom of gulch with hairpin turn. At top of gulch is a junction (at mile 15.3), easy to miss.

15.3　Junction. Turn LEFT to Mountain Home on Route 1566. You'll be leaving the main highway.

15.8　Mountain Home sign. Bed-and-breakfast amenities and camping but no automobile services.

18.1　Junction. Continue STRAIGHT. At mile 18.9 there are two sharp turns.

23.2　Junction. Turn RIGHT onto a dirt road following signs to Yellowstone Recreation Area (Moon Lake Recreation Area goes straight). You'll cross a single-lane bridge.

23.6　Junction on other side of bridge. Turn LEFT (a road to Altonah and Altamont goes right).

27.7　Junction. Turn RIGHT, following signs to Yellowstone (road to Hells Canyon goes left).

29.5　Start rough descent, 10-15 mph, after which you'll pass by Yellowstone Campground on left.

30.1　Pass by Bridge Campground on left, and cross one-lane bridge over Yellowstone River.

30.2　Junction. Turn LEFT, following the sign to Swift Creek (road to Hydro Power Plant goes right).

31.0　Junction. Continue STRAIGHT to Swift Creek (road to Dry Gulch goes left). Better road, 25-30 mph.

32.5　Reservoir Campground; Riverview Campground is at mile 32.7.

34.7　TRAILHEAD and campground.

Swift Creek Trailhead: The campground-trailhead area has eleven campsites with tables, grills, tap water, and pit toilets; fees are collected. There is a plethora of established campgrounds along the way, so car-camping pullouts are not common. But with the amenities provided by Swift Creek, there's no reason to camp anywhere else. See "Swift Creek Trail" description on page 124, "Yellowstone Creek Trail" description on page 102, and Map 13.

Uinta Trailhead (Atwood Basin Trail)

Take Highway 40 to downtown Roosevelt. If you're driving east, drive through the Lagoon Street stoplight. Then turn left (north) on 200 North (Highway 121). The road is paved for all but the last two miles, so it's a quick drive. You can generally just follow the signs to Uintah Canyon or U-Bar Ranch.

Estimated Driving Times:
    Salt Lake City to Roosevelt: 2 hours, 30 minutes
    Roosevelt to the trailhead: 45 minutes

0.0	Roosevelt.
10.4	Four-way stop in Neola. Go STRAIGHT to Uintah Canyon (Highway 121 goes right, to Vernal).
17.7	Junction. Continue STRAIGHT to Uintah Canyon (road to right goes to Elkhorn Whiterocks).
19.1	Y junction. Turn RIGHT to Uintah Canyon (the dirt road straight ahead goes to Yellowstone Trailhead).
23.2	Junction. Turn RIGHT to Uintah Canyon (going straight takes you to Big Spring Complex). You'll cross a two-lane bridge over the Uinta River.
23.5	Junction, immediately after the bridge. Turn LEFT to Uintah Canyon (the road to the right goes to Elkhorn Loop).
25.5	Pavement ends. 20–30 mph.
26.2	Uinta Canyon Campground entrance.
26.7	Uinta Group Use Area (reservation area) entrance. Continue STRAIGHT.
27.2	TRAILHEAD and parking for wilderness users.
27.7	Wandin Campground entrance.
27.8	TRAIL begins here. Day use–only parking area for fishermen. U-Bar Ranch private entrance straight ahead.

Uinta Trailhead: All campgrounds near the trailhead charge fees. They provide no tap water, so bring your own (the Uinta River is not convenient at all). They all have pit toilets and garbage pickup, including the trailhead parking area. Wandin Campground is small (about six sites). There is a handful of car-camping pullouts and side roads for about two miles before the trailhead parking, but most are in dusty sagebrush and ponderosa country. You could also probably crash for the night in the trailhead parking area, which is very large. See "Atwood Basin Trail" description on page 127 and Map 14.

The Kings-Emmons ridge, view from Pyramid Peak

Fortress Peak and Cliff Point, view from Henrys Fork basin

View of Upper Red Castle Lake from Wilson Peak

Kings Peak and South Kings Peak (skyline), view from Powell Saddle

Mount Lovenia, view from upper East Fork Blacks Fork basin

Gunsight Peak, Dome Peak, Fortress Peak, and Cliff Point, view from Island Lake, Henrys Fork basin

Wilson Peak, view from Smiths Fork Pass

GROUP 1: Blacks Fork Area Summits

- Mount Lovenia: 13,219 feet (#11)
- Tokewanna Peak: 13,165 feet (#13)
- Wasatch Peak: 13,156 feet (#15)
- Mount Wapiti (AN): 13,039 feet (#20)
- Quandary Peak (AN): 13,032 feet (#21)

Like most summits in the northwest region of the Uintas, these are very rugged, and they're the most demanding of the 13ers. No "easy" routes here. Given this fact, it's interesting that they're among the lowest 13ers (all in the lower half). The Lovenia Loop (AN), a route consisting of Mount Lovenia and Quandary Peak, has the most continuously rough terrain of any in this book. Another distinguishing feature is that Tokewanna Peak, Wasatch Peak, and Mount Wapiti are the only 13ers north of the Uinta crest, and from the summit of Tokewanna, the northernmost peak, you have an excellent east-west panorama of the entire range.

The West Fork Blacks Fork Trail and the East Fork Blacks Fork Trail (see Map 3) are the two best ways to approach this group. The two trails meet at Red Knob Pass. From either trail, you'll enjoy narrow glacier-carved drainages with craggy peaks on each side. Both basins are rich with wildlife, and elk, deer, moose, marmots, and grouse are commonly seen. There is a greater chance for solitude because these areas aren't visited as frequently as other places in the Uintas. One major attraction to the West Fork Blacks Fork approach is emerald-green Dead Horse Lake, nestled against the sheer Uinta crest. Those attractions also make it a more popular destination than the East Fork. I admit I wasn't expecting to put the East Fork basin on my favorites list, because like most people I gravitate toward Uinta lakes, and the East Fork is almost devoid of them. But after spending several days there in early July, I was amazed at the upper-basin area. Early-summer moisture creates gorgeous green high meadows that are accented with many wildflowers such as the tiny purple-pink alpine laurel and yellow cinquefoil. Mount Lovenia's craggy, reddish face is crisply defined by residual snowfields and makes an impressive backdrop to the vast meadow.

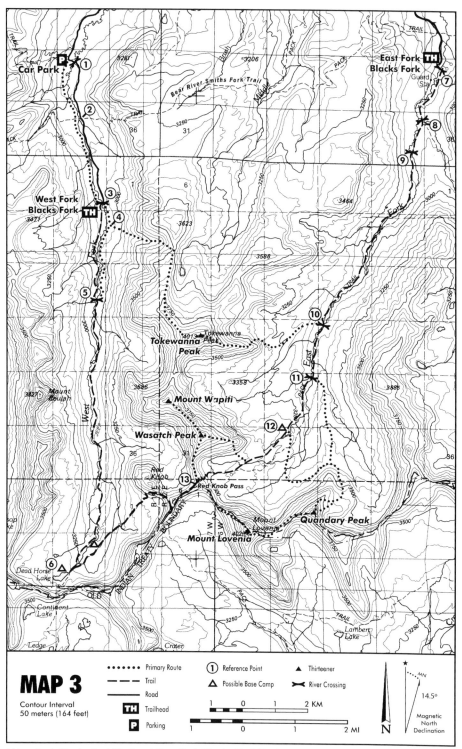

MAP 3

Contour Interval
50 meters (164 feet)

•••••• Primary Route
– – – Trail
——— Road
TH Trailhead
P Parking

① Reference Point
△ Possible Base Camp

▲ Thirteener
✕ River Crossing

Car Park
West Fork Blacks Fork **TH**
East Fork Blacks Fork **TH**
Guard Sta.

Bear River-Smiths Fork Trail

Tokewanna Peak
Mount Beulah
Mount Wapiti
Wasatch Peak
Red Knob
Red Knob Pass
Mount Lovenia
Quandary Peak
Dead Horse Lake
Continent Lake
Ledge
Crater
Lambert Lake

INDIAN TREATY BOUNDARY
OLD

1 0 1 2 KM
1 0 1 2 MI

N

MN
14.5°
Magnetic North Declination

West Fork Blacks Fork Trail and East Fork Blacks Fork Trail

For Tokewanna Peak, I've described two different routes, one from each trail (see Maps 4 and 5). They're both good routes, but the West Fork side is less rough. Wasatch Peak–Mount Wapiti and Mount Lovenia can be climbed starting from the trail at Red Knob Pass. Mount Wapiti—one of the more awkward 13ers to access—is approached here via the ridge from Wasatch, letting you climb two peaks in one starting from a high trail. Consider doing Wasatch and Wapiti together in one day, and Lovenia another day (ideally with Quandary). Coming from the East Fork, you can make a rewarding and challenging climb of Quandary Peak and Mount Lovenia (the Lovenia Loop).

One thing to consider is that doing the Red Knob Pass peaks from Dead Horse Lake is harder than from the East Fork side (it adds 2.6 more miles and 800 feet more climbing, round-trip). Camping closer to Red Knob Pass would equalize the two approaches. Even so, Quandary Peak will be more difficult, because you either have to do the rough Lovenia-Quandary ridge twice (out and back) or have to drop down into the East Fork basin. Alternatively, you could make a separate quick trip up the East Fork and do Quandary (or Quandary-Lovenia).

Estimated Time for an All-Inclusive Trip: four to six days (not including rest days, bad weather days, or driving time)

Trailhead Information

Driving directions and parking and campground information are detailed in the "Driving to the Trailheads" section. There are two main routes to the Blacks Fork trailheads—one starts from I-80 in Wyoming (see page 39), and the other uses the North Slope Road (see page 47) from Highway 150 in Utah.

Trail and Round-Trip Route Summaries

West Fork Blacks Fork Trail (Map 3)

TRAILHEAD: West Fork Blacks Fork Car Park, Elev. 9,300'
TIME ESTIMATE: 6.5 hrs to Dead Horse Lake

Destination (one-way)	Miles	Elevation	Elev. Gain
Start Tokewanna Peak Route (M3.3)	3.0	9,600'	+300'
Dead Horse Lake (M3.6)	10.4	10,880'	+1,580'
Red Knob Pass (M3.13)	14.0	12,165'	+3,265'–400'

East Fork Blacks Fork Trail (Map 3)

TRAILHEAD: East Fork Blacks Fork, Elev. 9,260'
TIME ESTIMATE: 5.5 hrs to upper-basin camping area (M3.12)

Destination (one-way)	Miles	Elevation	Elev. Gain
Start Tokewanna Peak Route (M3.10)	5.8	10,000'	+740'
Start Alt. Quandary Peak Route (M3.11)	6.9	10,160'	+900'
Upper-basin camping area (M3.12)	8.1	10,850'	+1,590'
Red Knob Pass (M3.13)	10.4	12,165'	+2,905'

Round-Trip Routes

Peaks: Starting Point	Elev. Gain	Miles	Time Est.	Grade
Tokewanna Peak (Map 5)				
East Fork Trail, 4th river crossing (M5.1)	+3,165'	5.7	6 hrs	III
TRAILHEAD (East Fork—M3.7)	+3,905'	17.3	—	—
Tokewanna Peak (Map 4)				
End West Fork primitive road (M4.1)	+3,585'	8.0	5.5 hrs	III
TRAILHEAD (West Fork—M3.1)	+3,905'	14.0	—	—
Wasatch, Wapiti (Map 6)				
Upper East Fork camping area (M6.1)*	+3,185'	7.5	7.5 hrs	III
Dead Horse Lake (M6)	+4,035'	11.2	9 hrs	IV
*TRAILHEAD (East Fork—M3.7)**	+4,775'	23.7	—	—
TRAILHEAD (West Fork—M3.1)	+5,615'	32.0	—	—
Wasatch Peak (Map 6)				
Upper East Fork camping area (M6.1)*	+2,385'	5.5	5 hrs	II
Dead Horse Lake (M6)	+3,235'	9.2	6.5 hrs	III
*TRAILHEAD (East Fork—M3.7)**	+3,975'	21.7	—	—
TRAILHEAD (West Fork—M3.1)	+4,815'	30.0	—	—
Quandary Peak (Map 7)				
Lower East Fork Trail (M7.11)	+2,850'	6.4	7 hrs	III
TRAILHEAD (East Fork—M3.7)	+3,790'	20.2	—	—
Quandary, Lovenia (Map 7)				
Upper East Fork camping area (M7.1)	+3,460'	8.7	9 hrs	IV
Dead Horse Lake (M6)	+5,880'	13.2	12 hrs	V
TRAILHEAD (East Fork—M3.7)	+5,050'	24.9	—	—
TRAILHEAD (West Fork—M3.1)	+7,460'	34.0	—	—
Mount Lovenia (Map 7)				
Upper East Fork camping area (M7.1)	+3,020'	7.6	5.5 hrs	III
Dead Horse Lake (M6)	+3,790'	10.2	7 hrs	IV
TRAILHEAD (East Fork—M3.7)	+4,610'	23.8	—	—
TRAILHEAD (West Fork—M3.1)	+5,370'	31.0	—	—
Wasatch, Wapiti, Lovenia (Maps 6, 7)				
Upper East Fork camping area (M6.1)	+4,970'	11.6	10.5 hrs	V
Dead Horse Lake (M6)	+5,740'	14.2	11.5 hrs	V
TRAILHEAD (East Fork—M3.7)	+6,560'	27.8	—	—
TRAILHEAD (West Fork—M3.1)	+7,320'	35.0	—	—

*Ascend via Red Knob Pass; descend via eastern ridge of Wasatch (M6.6).

West Fork Blacks Fork (Dead Horse Lake) Trail

Map point	M3.2	M3.3	M3.4	M3.5	M3.6	M3.13
Miles from trailhead	1.2	3.0	3.3	4.7	10.4	14.0

The West Fork Blacks Fork Trail is quite flat and easy to hike, and has a plethora of good camping spots (always with convenient access to the West Fork Blacks Fork River). The trail joins with the Highline Trail in the upper basin. The Highline Trail climbs southwest to Dead Horse Lake (M3.6) and continues northeast to Red Knob Pass (M3.13).

The directions presented here begin at the Car Park (M3.1), immediately before the first crossing of West Fork Blacks Fork. The actual hiking trail starts three miles up from the Car Park, but a bad stream crossing and rougher roads after the crossing make this a sensible starting point. Also, according to Forest Service maps, this is the trailhead (trail #101).

Following the primitive road from the Car Park, you'll have to immediately cross the river. In this part of the valley, the creek meanders through wide-open meadows and marshes, so your chances are slim to none of finding a handy log to cross the river on. But you can avoid this crossing, as well as the next one, by going cross-country (see "Cross-Country Options" following this section).

On the other side of the crossing, the road leaves the meadow and enters the forest. The road splits a couple of times, but all roads go to the same place if you keep heading upstream. You'll cross the Bear River Smiths Fork Trail (M3.2), which runs east-west along the north slope of the Uintas, about thirty minutes from the Car Park. Approximately forty minutes from the Bear River Smiths Fork Trail, you'll pass through another log fence, and shortly thereafter you'll reach the second stream crossing (M3.3).

If you're aiming for Tokewanna Peak, continue walking upstream (see "Cross-Country Segment 2" in the "Cross-Country Options" section below). Otherwise, dig out your wading shoes for the river crossing. It's doubtful you'll find any logs or boulders to hop across on. (If you've somehow made it to this point in your four-wheel-drive vehicle using the primitive-road route, it's worth pointing out that this crossing is better because it's quite rocky instead of sandy like the first crossing.)

On the other side of this crossing, it's just a one-minute walk through a meadow to the hiking trailhead, where the road ends. There's a trail register at a log fence, and a convenient but simplistic wood-burn map of the West Fork area.

The wilderness boundary is about five minutes up the trail. About one mile from the wilderness boundary the trail begins following very close to the river, at the edge of Buck Pasture. A couple of minutes alongside the meadow, look-ing up ahead, you'll see a log fence line that crosses the river. Where it spans the river, a couple of big logs have been sheared to make a very sturdy, handy single-person footbridge (M3.5).

Despite cairns and markers you might see early on, taking a direct line to the bridge across the meadows isn't advisable due to marshy terrain. Instead, continue walking—the trail will pass through the fence line in the trees, and end up closer to the bridge (perhaps seventy feet away), where you can pick a nonboggy path to the river's edge. A trail of sorts may keep going, but the main trail goes across the footbridge.

Several minutes from the footbridge, you'll pass by a rotting cabin near its last breath—the roof has long since caved in, and a tree has fallen with perfect aim across the middle, breaking the tree in two and almost knocking the cabin over.

The Uinta crest and upper basin get more and more incredible the farther you hike. The craggy west ridge, which features the imposing Mount Beulah at 12,553 feet, rivals anything you'll see in the Rockies. As you approach the upper basin, keep in mind that Dead Horse Lake doesn't sit in the middle of the basin like you might expect, but instead is higher and to the right.

About two miles before Dead Horse Lake, you'll start gaining elevation more quickly. You'll again cross the river about a mile and a quarter before the lake. However, the river is much smaller by now, just one of the tributaries, making a boulder-hop crossing a good possibility.

The trail crosses the West Fork for the final time about a quarter mile from the lake. Immediately afterward, the West Fork Trail ends at the intersection with the Highline Trail (#025 on Forest Service maps). Go right, following the Highline Trail up a steep, tiring slope to Dead Horse Lake (M3.6). Going left on the Highline Trail takes you to Red Knob Pass.

The best camping at Dead Horse Lake is on the north side. You can cross the outlet stream on boulders. The camping spots get more and more sparse and rocky the farther you walk west. Be sure to camp as far away from the lakeshore as possible. Dead Horse Lake is heavily used—virtually everyone who comes into the upper basin will camp at this lake. The Forest Service is monitoring the area for possible permanent fire prohibitions. For these rea-sons, consider moving closer to the peaks, by walking east down the Highline Trail, toward Red Knob Pass, instead of going up to Dead Horse Lake.

Route Segment	Miles	Gain/Loss	Time Est.
Dead Horse Lake to Red Knob Pass (Map 6)	3.6	+1,685'/-400'	2 hrs

From Dead Horse Lake, the Highline Trail drops about four hundred feet in elevation on its way northeast to Red Knob Pass. Where it reaches the lowest point, about three-quarters of a mile from Dead Horse Lake, there are some open grassy areas with possible camping below the trail (see Map 3). There should be a small stream to get water from that flows down through the grassy swale.

The trail traverses up through the timber on increasingly inclined slopes. You'll cross another small stream near timberline, with sloped campsite possibilities. The trail then enters the meadow below the pass, where you can follow cairns or simply head across the meadow toward the pass.

You'll see the trail cutting across the slope beneath Red Knob (which, by the way, really is kind of red and knobby looking). The trail tops out on the saddle (M6.7) just south of Red Knob. It turns south, going just below the ridge for one-third of a mile to the "official" Red Knob Pass, where a trail (M6.8) drops down into Lake Fork.

Follow the trail along the ridge to the eastern end of the pass. The routes to Wasatch Peak–Mount Wapiti and Mount Lovenia–Quandary Peak leave the trail just before it drops down into the East Fork Blacks Fork (see M3.13, M6.2, and M7.10).

CROSS-COUNTRY OPTIONS FOR THE WEST FORK BLACKS FORK TRAIL

The flat West Fork basin floor is very well suited to cross-country hiking. If you're going straight to Dead Horse Lake, you can skip the first two river crossings by using Cross-Country Segment 1. It's well worth considering if the water levels are high (in early season) or freezing cold (in the fall). If you're climbing Tokewanna Peak, you'll be using Cross-Country Segment 2 (or at least part of it).

Cross-Country Segment 1: From the Car Park (M3.1) to the Hiking Trailhead and Second River Crossing (M3.3)

This route follows the west side of the rive. Most of the route is on level ground, with surprisingly little deadfall and simple route-finding. The West Fork valley is basically a big boggy marsh for the first mile, so your best bet is to stay away from the river and walk at the edge of the forest. For a short distance you can actually follow a faint trail that leaves the car park area. As soon as the marshes disappear, veer back to the river's edge where the hiking and navigation are much easier. On your way to the hiking trailhead, you will pass through two old, worn-down log fences. You'll also cross the Bear River Smiths Fork Trail, but it's faint so you might not notice it. Eventually, you'll meet up with the primitive road in a large meadow. The hiking trailhead is only a minute's walk up the road, at a log fence, where the road ends. Note that the road has just crossed the river (M3.3).

Cross-Country Segment 2: Continuing Upstream from the Second Crossing (M3.3)

On the east side of the second crossing (M3.3), begin walking upstream on easy terrain near the river's edge.

To climb Tokewanna Peak, leave the riverside after a short ten-minute walk and start climbing left (east) up the timbered slopes (M3.4). Read the "Toke-wanna Peak from West Fork Blacks Fork" route description for more details.

If you continue walking cross-country upstream, you will eventually (in thirty to forty minutes) reach the main trail after it crosses the footbridge (M3.5) in upper Buck Pasture. Staying near or within sight of the river, this route is just as easy as walking on the official hiking trail. In fact, you can follow faint trails much of the way, and you'll even see some tree blazes. There are also many places to camp, more so than the trail side of the river, which is rockier.

East Fork Blacks Fork Trail

Map point	M3.8	M3.9	M3.10	M3.11	M3.12	M3.13
Miles from trailhead	1.3	2.0	5.8	6.9	8.1	10.5

The East Fork Blacks Fork Trail (#102 on Forest Service maps) begins where the road curves uphill into the campground, just before the bulletin board. The trail drops immediately down to the river, which it crosses (M3.7) on a sturdy bridge (the only real bridge on the trail). In just a few minutes, you'll come to a trail junction. Go right on the East Fork Trail.

In about a mile you'll cross three small side streams, then a marsh with a board walkway. Soon after, you'll come to Little East Fork (M3.8), the first of the main stream crossings along the trail. Here the stream has split into two parts, one small and one large, both of which are easily crossed on logs.

Immediately after the crossing is the junction with the Little East Fork Trail, which goes left, but is hard to see initially. Continue straight ahead on the East Fork Blacks Fork Trail. (A sign indicates that by hiking straight ahead you're headed for Dead Horse Lake, which is a bit strange because it's not in this basin—you have to hike over Red Knob Pass into the West Fork to get to it.)

The next half mile or so has some particularly excellent camping spots in flat, shady meadows, with the river close by. About ten minutes after passing a

Brent DeHaan hikes toward Mount Lovenia on the East Fork Trail

crumbling shell of a cabin, you'll reach the next major river crossing (M3.9). You *might* find a bridge at the river crossing, but flooding had destroyed the bridge at the time of this writing. However, this portion of the river is wide and shallow, which makes it fairly easy to wade.

A long, broad meadow with scattered clusters of tall willows begins immediately on the other side of the river. The open meadow provides a view of one of the 13ers rising above the treetops. Nearing the end of the meadow is the wilderness boundary, marked by a sign. It should be noted that most maps erroneously show the trail crossing the river shortly after the wilderness boundary, only to cross again about a mile later. The trail now avoids these crossings by staying on the west side of the river.

The trail so far has been a very gentle uphill climb, almost level in places. Now, as you enter the forest again, you'll climb up a few brief steeper sections. On one of the hilly rises, you'll catch the first view of all five of the basin's 13ers, seen through lodgepole trunks.

About three and a half miles past the wilderness boundary, you'll come to the fourth big stream crossing (M3.10), about six miles from the trailhead. If you're climbing Tokewanna Peak's eastern ridge, leave the trail here and head west (see "Tokewanna Peak, from East Fork Blacks Fork" description on page 65). You can't actually see the peak due to thick timber, so this crossing serves as a landmark; it is distinctive because the trail crosses at the tip of a miniature forested island in the middle of the stream. If for some reason you want to see Tokewanna Peak, you'll have to ford the river and walk northeast into the meadow on the other side.

Just over a mile later you'll cross the East Fork for the last time (M3.11). The river here is much smaller and is nicely spanned by two solid logs. On the other side, the trail starts contouring steeply uphill, gaining elevation quickly.

This last stream crossing (M3.11) and sudden uphill section is another landmark—this is the takeoff point for a possible route to Quandary Peak (see page 76). But if you're out to bag other peaks on this trip, you'll probably want to continue up the trail to a higher base camp.

Heading up the trail, you'll go nearly straight up the steep, forested slope for a half mile before the trail tops out at the edge of a marshy meadow. Tokewanna Peak rises above the dense trees that surround the marsh. Shortly thereafter, the trail will have *another* straight-up-the-slope section before topping out on a shelf high above the river.

About fifteen minutes after the trail tops out, you'll enter a large meadow. This meadow is very scenic, with a stream running through it and a rather picturesque isolated tree and boulder by the trail, and is a good base-camping area (see M3.12, M6.1, and M7.1). Not much higher from this point the ground gets steeper and is exposed above timberline.

Route Segment	Miles	Gain/Loss	Time Est.
Upper-basin camping area (M6.1, M7.1) to Red Knob Pass	2.3	+1,315	1.5 hrs

Hike another twenty minutes or so up the trail, and you'll rise above timberline and enter the vast upper-basin meadow between Lovenia and Wasatch. It's a beautiful plateaulike area, filled with wildflowers in early summer, and spring-fed streams meandering down from the base of Red Knob Pass. The trail through the meadow is well defined. After a handful of nice switchbacks, you'll arrive at the eastern end of Red Knob Pass (see M3.13, M6.2, and M7.10). The "official" Red Knob Pass as labeled on USGS maps is three-quarters of a mile farther west.

Tokewanna Peak, from West Fork Blacks Fork

One-way Route Summary

Reference	Miles	Gain/Loss	Time Est.	Class
Map 4, P1	4.0	+3,585'	3.5 hrs	2+

This route starts near the end of the primitive road in West Fork, climbs east up to Bob's Saddle (AN), and follows the ridgeline to the summit. Tokewanna is probably the easiest 13er to climb in a one-day trip from your vehicle, at only eight miles round-trip from the end of the primitive road, or fourteen miles round-trip from the Car Park (M3.1).

First, make your way to the second stream crossing near the end of the primitive road (M4.1 and M3.3). Refer to the "West Fork Blacks Fork Trail" description for details. Start by walking upstream (south). You'll soon walk into meadows where you'll have a better view of where you're headed. As you walk, look to your left (east) and you'll see two high points on the ridge—the Twin Knolls (AN) (see Map 4). Bob's Saddle is the lowest point to the right (south) of the Twin Knolls.

In 0.4 miles (around ten minutes, depending on your pace) from where you left the primitive road, you should see an isolated group of mostly dead trees (M4.2) in the middle of the meadow. Bob's Saddle is at a compass bearing of exactly ninety degrees (with no declination adjustments) from this tree cluster. Leave the meadows here and begin walking east toward the saddle.

You'll soon enter the forest, losing your view of the ridge above. The first slopes are Class 1+ with a small amount of deadfall. The slope quickly gets much steeper (CL 2). You should end up climbing on the right-hand side of a gully containing a small stream (the left-hand side of the gully has rougher terrain).

In about thirty minutes (roughly 0.75 miles), you'll start to see talus or boulder fields on the slopes on either side. The deep gully disappears here, along with the water, depending on the season. From here you could walk in the bottom of the drainage (CL 1+), or you could veer left and walk at the base of the rocky slopes, a rather nice natural pathway that avoids most of the deadfall.

Approximately twenty minutes later, the drainage essentially comes to an end in a very steep, bowl-like area (M4.3), where the forest thins out. Veer a little to the right as you climb upslope through loose talus, scree, dirt, and patchy vegetation (CL 2+). The slope angle eases up in ten to twenty minutes, after which it's a nice Class 1+ climb on alpine vegetation and grass to Bob's Saddle.

The saddle is grassy, rolling, and beautiful. At this point, you've climbed half the vertical elevation to the summit. To the south, an easygoing, undulating ridge top leads to Tokewanna Peak. It's a long, exposed ridge (2.2 miles), so plan ahead to avoid getting caught by a thunderstorm.

Begin walking south from Bob's Saddle along the ridge top. The ridge is mostly vegetated and has flat to low-angled Class 1 to 1+ terrain most of the way to the summit. After USGS elevation point 12412, you'll start along a fabulous narrow ridge with sweeping views to either side. You can look to the right

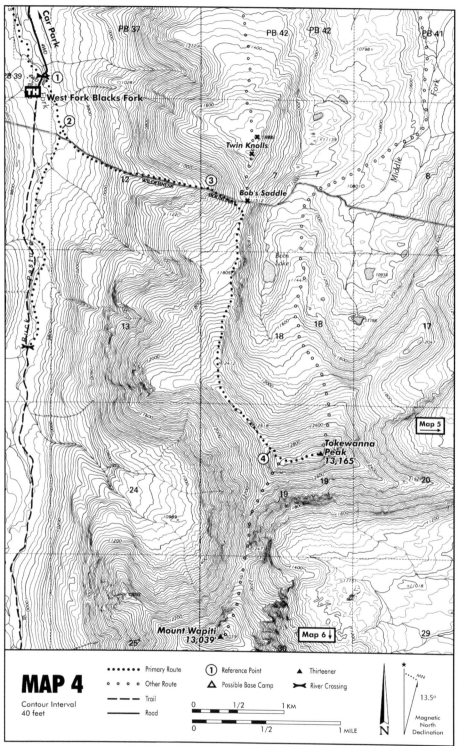

MAP 4

Contour Interval
40 feet

Primary Route
○ ○ ○ ○ Other Route
– – – Trail
——— Road

① Reference Point
△ Possible Base Camp

▲ Thirteener
✕ River Crossing

0   1/2   1 KM

0   1/2   1 MILE

N

13.5°

Magnetic
North
Declination

Tokewanna, from West Fork Blacks Fork

Ray Overson and David Rose on the summit of Tokewanna Peak

into the massive cirque between Tokewanna and Mount Wapiti, or left into the gentler Middle Fork.

Upon reaching the summit block (M4.4), the easy ridge ends, and you'll start climbing a steep, bouldered slope (CL 2+). If you swing a little to the left onto Tokewanna's northern slopes, the angle is easier. After climbing up this slope for about fifteen minutes, you'll reach the summit ridge top, with a one-third-mile mild boulder-hop to the summit.

The summit of Tokewanna Peak has a rugged south side, with thirty-foot drop-offs. It has a summit register (an indication of this mountain's popularity) in the usual old metal mailbox. If you've been curious about the origin of the name Tokewanna, a registry entry by Lanera Grondel and Dick Wilson, dated August 16, 1993, should be interesting: "Tokewanna was named by Native Americans—at least 6 tribes used the same word. The Hebrew definition means Peace—He who was pierced in the palm of the hand."

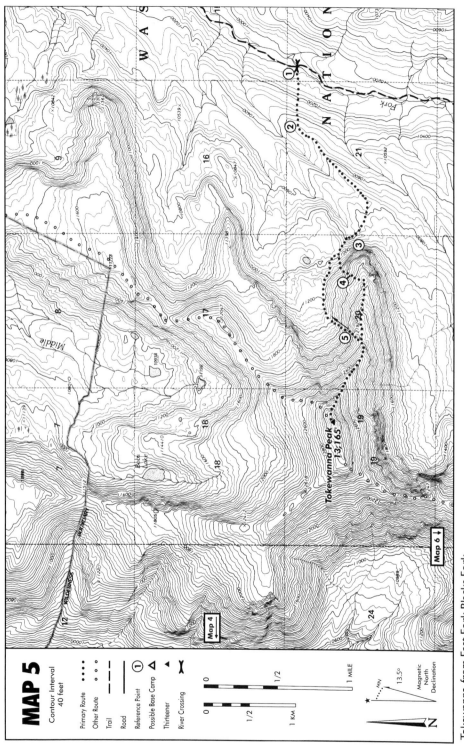

Map 4

Map 6 ↓

Tokewanna, from East Fork Blacks Fork

Tokewanna Peak, view from Wasatch Peak

Tokewanna Peak, from East Fork Blacks Fork
One-way Route Summary

Reference	Miles	Gain/Loss	Time Est.	Class
Map 5, P1	2.8	+3,165'	3.5-4 hrs	3+

Typically, routes described in this book begin above or near timberline, but this route is unique in that the first half of the route goes through dense forest. To avoid navigation problems, follow the map closely. Also, assuming you'll be heading back to your cached packs at the East Fork River, it helps to take mental note of landmarks on the opposite side of the drainage. In general, this route is rougher and more demanding than it looks.

To reach the beginning of this route, first read the details in the "East Fork Blacks Fork Trail" description. Leave the East Fork Trail at the "island" river crossing (M5.1 and M3.10) and start walking west directly toward Tokewanna Peak (248 degrees compass bearing, without any declination adjustments).

Walking through the forest, you'll almost immediately begin climbing a very steep, partially vegetated Class 1+ slope. After perhaps fifteen minutes, you'll top out on a minor rounded ridge (M5.2), still in the forest. Turn left (southwest) and hike along the top. At some point, a distant spur peak of Tokewanna becomes visible to your right (west). Not to be confused with Tokewanna, it's recognizable by nearby reddish rock layers. About ten minutes along the ridge, the forest opens up more, and to the south, you can see

Quandary Peak high in the East Fork basin. You'll start to encounter some deadfall, making progress a bit slower.

Eventually, you should see the large, bulky cliffed buttress that marks the end of Tokewanna Peak's eastern ridge. Veer to your right toward the base (M5.3) of the buttress. You will cross a shallow swale and another little ridge before arriving at the bottom of a boulder field at the base of the buttress. From here you still have the bulk of the climb ahead, more than twenty-three hundred feet and one and one-half miles to go. Go up a steep swale to the right of the boulder field and buttress, passing through some enormous boulders.

After reaching the top of the swale and rounding the corner, the buttress's cliffs will break up, creating some doable but very steep routes (M5.4), about Class 2, up to the ridge crest. A good route goes straight up, just to the right (west) of a solitary fifteen-foot-high block of rock, a residual part of the cliffs. Most of the route has consolidated soil and grass patches you can strategically use to make climbing easier. Climbing for just a few minutes, you'll have a view of a beautiful waterfall about a half mile to the north. It cascades about four hundred feet down the cirque's northern escarpment.

Once you reach the ridge top, simply follow it west toward the summit. It's an interesting ridge, with a lot of climbing variety and some surprisingly rough sections. The first half of the ridge top is quite varied in difficulty, from Class 1 to 2+. In the second half, you'll pass through two really interesting geologic areas with multicolored layers of square and angular rocks and strikingly smooth soil. A short Class 2+ or 3 section separates the two areas.

Finally, after a bit of Class 1–2 climbing, you'll reach the last leg to the summit. It's the roughest part of the ridge (CL 3 to 3+ scramble, depending on the route) with some shifty boulders thrown in for good measure. After the scramble, it's just a few more minutes of walking on wobbly boulders (CL 1+ or 2) to reach the summit.

Alternative Descent to East Fork Blacks Fork Trail

As you descend Tokewanna, you may be interested in an alternative (and fast) route (M5.5) down the eastern ridge. Keep an eye out for a wide, greenish, smooth-looking slope that starts halfway down the ridge top and extends to the left (north) almost all the way down to the cirque floor. This steep slope is initially composed of loose soil and small rocks, making descent easy. It has some potentially hazardous sections near the bottom where very hard and steep surfaces make secure footing difficult (effectively CL 2+). It'll probably take you only about fifteen minutes to descend more than eight hundred feet (minus a

Ray Overson on Wasatch-Wapiti ridge (Wasatch top right)

few minutes emptying dirt out of your shoes!). At the bottom, you'll want to make your way back to the base of the eastern ridge buttress (M5.3). To get there, you can follow an easy (CL 1 to 1+) pathlike route between the lateral moraines that parallel the eastern ridge. You might also find some game trails to follow.

Whatever your descent route, once you have arrived back at the base of the buttress (M5.3), you'll have to rely on your map and landmarks to navigate through the forest and back to the East Fork River "Island" trail crossing (M5.1). When you reach the river, common sense says that if you don't see the trail, walk downstream (north) to the crossing; if you *do* stumble across the trail, walk on the trail upstream (south) to the crossing. The descent from the summit to the East Fork Trail will take about two and a half hours.

Wasatch Peak, from Red Knob Pass

One-way Route Summary

Reference	Miles	Gain/Loss	Time Est.	Class
Map 6, P2	1.0	+1,070/-80	1.5 hrs	2+

The route starts at the eastern end of Red Knob Pass, leaving the trail and going north to the summit. From there, you can climb Mount Wapiti by continuing northwest along the ridge. An alternative route for descent or ascent follows the eastern ridge of Wasatch Peak.

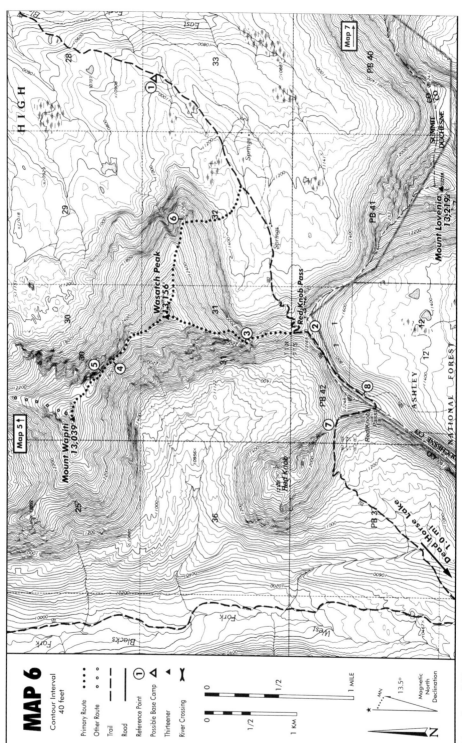

MAP 6

Contour Interval
40 feet

Primary Route •••••••

Other Route ○○○○○○

Trail – – – – – – –

Road ─────

① Reference Point

△ Possible Base Camp

▲ Thirteener

✕ River Crossing

0   1/2   1 KM

0   1/2   1 MILE

N

13.5°
Magnetic North
Declination

Wasatch and Wapiti

Wasatch Peak (center skyline), view from Wasatch-Wapiti ridge

From the eastern end of Red Knob Pass (M6.2), head north along the ridge toward Wasatch Peak. Stay on or near the ridge top, a Class 1 to 1+ climb that goes over a couple of humps. Shortly before reaching the base of Wasatch Peak, the ridge becomes craggy and broken. You can bypass this area on the right-hand (east) side by traversing beneath it on a loose dirt and debris spillway (CL 2+) coming from the crags above.

When you reach the base of Wasatch Peak at a small saddle, you'll encounter a system of cliffs (M6.3). It's an obstacle that you can't fully anticipate when viewing the route from below. If you go around the cliffs to the left (west), there's a Class 5 rock climb up at least one or more cliff bands. Instead, go to the right (east) side. It goes between the cliff's rock layers, following a narrow shelf walkway (a carefully done CL 1+ traverse). The walkway begins about ten feet vertically higher than the lowest part of the saddle. In spite of how it might look at first glance, you'll soon discover that the route isn't difficult. You should be able to walk on stable terrain by climbing on top of any rock-slide debris while simultaneously staying within arm's reach of the rock wall as you go. After a half-dozen steps or so, you're past the worst part. The entire traverse of the walkway is short, perhaps a few minutes. Afterward, the cliffs break up enough to start going upward again. Take mental note of where you exited the cliff traverse, if you're returning this way.

Angle up and through small broken rock bands on Wasatch Peak's south face (generally CL 2). Initially, the slope has some loose dirt and scattered boulders, but generally the slope is stable and anchored by grass clumps, making climbing fairly easy. Eventually, the rock bands give way to the standard Uinta boulder fields. You could continue up the face, but the ridge-top climbing is easier (CL 1+ to 2)—the incline is less, and it has more stable, consolidated terrain. You'll know you're nearing the summit when the slope angle increases and you start scrambling over larger, somewhat shifty boulders.

The weathered remains of a collapsed wood triangulation station sit atop the summit. Survey markers embedded into the rock in 1962 officially name the peak Wasatch. From here you have a grand view of all the 13ers except Dome Peak. Gunsight Peak is barely distinguishable as it peeks over Mount Powell.

Wasatch Peak Descent to Upper East Fork Blacks Fork

To	Miles	Gain/Loss	Time Est.	Class
Upper East Fork camping area (M6.1)	2.2	-2,305'	2 hrs	2+

To trail: 1.2 miles, -1,955', 1.5 hrs

For a shorter trip (by about one mile) back to the East Fork Blacks Fork Trail, take the eastern ridge of Wasatch. The route goes down the ridge and drops down to the basin just before reaching USGS elevation point 12268 (M6.6). Using this descent route, you could make a loop climb of Wasatch (and include Mount Wapiti if desired).

The first five to ten minutes of the descent has a steep Class 2+ section before reaching a flat area; from there, the ridge averages about Class 1+. Before about mid-July, you should find a low-angled snowfield covering a long section of the middle part of the ridge that you could glissade down. Near the end of the ridge, on the northern side, there's a wide, spectacular chute that plunges more than one thousand feet to the basin below. The East Fork has very few lakes, but the largest one is in view below the chute.

Eventually, you'll reach a rocky knoll (M6.6) on the eastern end of the ridge. Just before reaching this knoll, head down the face to your right (south), entering a slight swale. This is where the route turns ugly; it's a very steep, partially vegetated slope (CL 2+). You may encounter an early-season snowfield that runs down the swale; it gradually gets dangerously steep, so don't try it without an ice axe to control your descent. The slope on either side of the swale is very tiring.

This route is also a possibility for an ascent. It's more direct than going the Red Knob Pass route, but having experienced this tough slope firsthand, I'd probably opt for Red Knob Pass. If you do ascend this route, you can pick your way along intermittent vegetated sections, but for the most part it's going to be one-step-up, half-step-back-type climbing on loose terrain.

Mount Wapiti, from Wasatch Peak
One-way Route Summary

Reference	Miles	Gain/Loss	Time Est.	Class
Map 6	1.0	-450/+350	1–1.5 hrs	3

This is a grand and invigorating ridge route, with several scrambling sections. From Wasatch Peak, descend north along the ridge. It's slow going initially, a Class 3 scramble over larger, jagged boulders, until reaching the first low point on the connecting ridge at the bottom of the summit hump. This initial section from the summit might be made easier by staying just left of the ridge rather than on the crest. Continuing from the bottom of the summit hump, you'll be walking on moderate Class 1+ terrain, often with rugged drop-offs on the eastern side.

At about the halfway point, you'll reach a picturesque fifteen-foot-high rock protrusion coming out of a base of strangely greenish soil (M6.4). You'll have to climb up and around to the left (west) of the rock protrusion, and pick your way across a brief rough section of ridge. It's quite a scramble (CL 3). Alternatively, you could drop down to the left (west) beneath the rock protrusion, traverse beneath some cliffs, and climb steeply (CL 2) back up to the ridge top—more laborious but less rough. Whichever way you go, look downslope for a very interesting rock formation—there's a tall, slender rock spire that seems sure to collapse at any moment.

Mount Wapiti (skyline), view from Wasatch–Wapiti ridge

As you climb along the ridge, you'll have fabulous views of the east face, and increasing exposure. The eastern side of the ridge soon turns into an enormous three-hundred-foot wall. If you're on the very top of the ridge, you should come across a couple of nice viewpoints (M6.5). Beginning at this wall, a massive system of cliffs and buttresses cascades diagonally down the face in yellow, purplish, and brown layers. It's a breathtaking sight.

From the enormous wall viewpoint, the ridge top itself is suddenly but briefly very steep (CL 2+), in addition to the tremendous east-side exposure. Veer to the left (west), and you'll find an easier, less exposed, typical Uinta boulder-strewn slope. You'll go up a Class 2 section to a very broad, rounded knoll, a high point along the ridge.

The rest of the way to the peak is easy. Walk from the knoll along the flat, gentle ridge to the base of the summit mound, and climb up a Class 1+ slope to the summit. From the summit you have an excellent face-on view of Mount Beulah (to the west), one of the more distinct and imposing peaks around.

Quandary Peak, from Upper East Fork Blacks Fork
One-way Route Summary

Reference	Miles	Gain/Loss	Time Est.	Class
Map 7, P1	3.4	+2,185	3-4.5 hrs	3+ or 5

Starting from the upper-basin area (M7.1), this route goes to the base of Quandary, and then takes advantage of the topography by ascending a large portion of the peak on its relatively gentle eastern-northeastern slopes. Near the summit, the route splits into two tough routes (M7.5)—one route goes directly up the east face, the other up the northeast ridge. If you're doing the Lovenia Loop, you'll continue by going west along the ridge to Mount Lovenia and down to the trail at Red Knob Pass.

From the upper basin, make a semicontouring path around the top of the river valley (M7.2). By contouring, you can avoid the bigger bogs as well as inefficient elevation loss, but you could always try cutting straight east across the river valley. At the base of Quandary, follow natural terraces and game trails (CL 1) around to the northernmost point (M7.3). The "Quandary Peak, from Lower East Fork Blacks Fork" route (starting at M7.11) joins in here.

After rounding the northern point you may begin to see cairns. Look for a broad, rounded shoulder, truncated by broken cliffs on the mountain's northeast slopes (M7.4). The climbing route goes between this shoulder and Quandary Peak's northeast ridge. Cairns continue to mark much of the way,

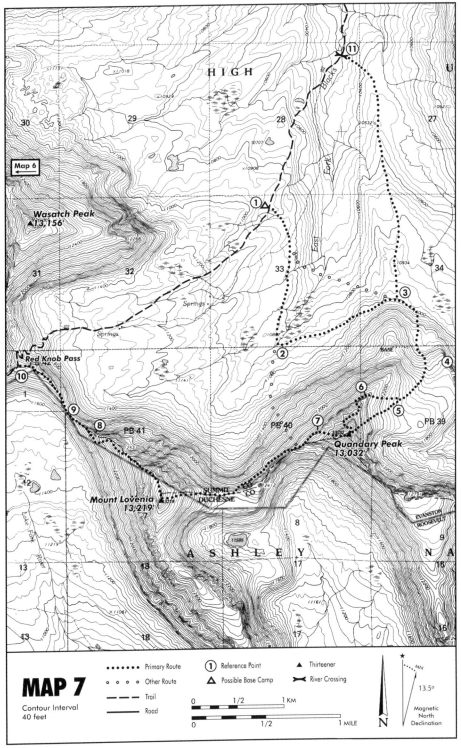

HIGH

Map 6

Wasatch Peak
▲13,156'

Springs

Springs

Red Knob Pass

Blacks

East Fork

BASE

Quandary Peak
13,032'

PB 41

PB 40

PB 39

Mount Lovenia
13,219'

SUMMIT CO
DUCHESNE CO

EVANSTON
ROOSEVELT

Lake Fork River

ASHLEY

NA

MAP 7

Contour Interval
40 feet

•••••• Primary Route

∘ ∘ ∘ ∘ Other Route

– – – Trail

——— Road

① Reference Point

△ Possible Base Camp

▲ Thirteener

⋈ River Crossing

0   1/2   1 KM

0   1/2   1 MILE

N

MN

13.5°

Magnetic
North
Declination

Quandary and Lovenia

Quandary Peak, view from Upper East Fork basin

but it's not entirely clear if they are indicating some kind of summit route. You'll begin climbing a vegetated, very high-angled slope (CL 2), topping out on a relatively small, flat shelf. In early summer, there's a scenic little waterfall going over broken rock strata on the far side of the shelf.

Climbing above the shelf, the mountain landscape opens up into broad, gentle, rolling terrain on the east side of the peak (M7.5). The easy climbing ends here, and you'll have a good perspective of the remaining 600-foot climb to the summit of Quandary. From here, there are two route options, both of them scrambles that negotiate some large, imposing cliff bands.

Option 1: The Summit via the Northeast Ridge, Class 3+

This route follows the ridge you can see on the skyline, but bypasses cliffs by traversing on the opposite side of the ridge (the northwest side, out of view from your vantage point). It's not as steep as route option 2 but involves steady scrambling and climbing over rugged terrain.

Looking at the skyline ridge from M7.5, you'll see two main cliff bands. The first cliff band circles beneath the summit (a sort of "summit cap"). The second one is farther down and creates a large, blocky shape against the skyline (M7.6). Make your way up to the base of that second cliff band, hiking up a mostly vegetated, stable slope.

When you reach the base of the cliff, begin a Class 1+ traverse beneath it, heading away from the ridge crest onto Quandary Peak's northwest slopes. It's easy if you stay within a few feet of the cliff, at the very base.

Shortly, you'll reach the first break in the cliffs, a gully or slide filled with unstable boulders. Start climbing up this slide (CL 2+), initially staying next to the rock face for stability. A little farther up, the break widens, and you can handily zigzag through a series of rock layers.

As soon as you can, make your way back to the ridge top and climb up to the next cliff band. Again, traverse beneath this cliff band to the right (west). The cliff isn't big, so you may quickly see a comfortable way to climb up (around ten to fifteen feet high, CL 4+ or 5); otherwise keep traversing, and you will pass along the top of two broad gullies, after which the cliff breaks up enough to start upward again.

Once above the cliff band, look for a wide break (maybe forty feet wide) in yet another band of cliffs. It's the last cliff band, an extension of the "summit cap" cliffs as seen from the eastern slopes of Quandary. Scramble up through the wide break (CL 2). You'll be on loose talus initially, but soon you can zigzag more easily along natural rock-shelf walkways.

Again make your way back to the ridge top. This is the final leg to the summit, a fairly short but very rugged Class 3 to 3+ scramble.

Option 2: The Summit via the East Face, Class 5

Looking up at Quandary from M7.5, you'll see a high, vertical cliff band that appears to ring the summit, creating a "summit cap." Just to the left of the center of the summit cap, there's a short couloir that breaks up the cliff band. The route goes up through this break. The entire route to the summit is on high-angled slopes, much steeper than the northeast ridge. In addition, until mid- to late summer the couloir itself is mostly filled with snow. Unless you are experienced and have snow-climbing equipment, don't try it until the snow has melted.

The slopes leading up to the couloir are fairly loose and steep, Class 2. Snow free, the hardest section of the gully or couloir is around Class 3+ or 4 for fifty feet with a ten-foot Class 5.3 rock climb at the crux—it's a fun climb for those who are up for a challenge beyond the typical Uinta route. After the couloir break, the remaining climb is simply a straight-up shot to the summit—it's a steep, tough scramble (CL 2+ or 3) on very loose dirt, scree, talus, and broken rock bands.

Quandary Peak, from Lower East Fork Blacks Fork

One-way Route Summary

Reference	Miles	Gain/Loss	Time Est.	Class
Map 7, P1 1	3.2	+2,850	4 hrs	3+ or 5

If you're coming from lower down on the East Fork Trail (versus from the up-per-basin camping area), this approach is the most direct way to get to Quandary Peak. The route starts at the trail's fifth and last stream crossing (M7.11 and M3.11). Read the "East Fork Blacks Fork Trail" description for de-tails. The route goes south, climbing the small, forested ridgeline that runs be-tween East Fork and the small subdrainage to the east. The first section of this route, to the base of Quandary Peak, is straightforward and doable, averaging an easy Class 1+. There is no heavy deadfall, and there are no surprises. You will be hiking through timber most of the way to the base of Quandary Peak, but it's easy to stay on course. The trees thin out as you get higher, offering in-creased views. If you stay on the ridge top, you'll avoid a few large side gullies on the right-hand (west) side, and have smoother hiking. The ridge top natu-rally connects to the northernmost point (M7.3) of Quandary Peak's base. From here, you'll connect with the route coming from the upper basin (see "Quandary Peak, from Upper East Fork Blacks Fork" on page 72).

Mount Lovenia, from Quandary Peak

One-way Route Summary

Reference	Miles	Gain/Loss	Time Est.	Class
Map 7	1.5	-1,140/+950	2-2.5 hrs	3

This daunting ridge route going west to Mount Lovenia is part of the Lovenia Loop. The ridge's middle section is a distinct, very narrow, flat-topped fin. It looks interesting, but, obviously, walking the actual ridge top is not a good idea due to cliffs and a couple of knife-edge sections. Instead, you can make a tire-some but reasonable traverse beneath the cliffs on the steep and loose northern slopes. It's a tough route made tougher because you'll lose more than one thousand feet in elevation along the way.

From the summit of Quandary Peak, start west down the ridge top. After a minute or two, leave the ridge crest and angle down the northwest face on loose talus (CL 2). The face becomes a wide depression that steepens and narrows somewhat as it funnels you closer to a long cliff band. You should reach a break in the cliff, where you can slither down an eight-foot Class 4 crack (M7.7).

Ray Overson heads to Mount Lovenia from Quandary Peak

Once you get below the cliffs, make a descending traverse back to the ridge top. Continuing down the ridge top, you'll come to another cliff band. Bypass it by dropping down to the right (north), which should bring you to the low point of the ridge.

From the low point, begin a traverse toward Lovenia (CL 2+ to 3). The slopes are very steep, consisting mostly of loose soil with scattered boulders, and a few sections of more typical Uinta talus. The traverse is only about a half mile long, but due to the loose terrain it will probably take a fatiguing forty-five minutes to an hour.

Just before connecting to Mount Lovenia, the cliffs above you come to an end. Climb up a boulder field to the saddle. You've got it made now—the ridge from the saddle to the summit of Mount Lovenia is relatively easy (CL 2) and will take approximately one hour. You'll be climbing mostly on grass and soil patches and very stable boulders.

Atop Mount Lovenia's broad summit, there's a remarkably unobstructed view of the famed Mount Timpanogos. Although it's located in the Wasatch Range more than sixty miles away, on a clear day its shape is amazingly recognizable.

Mount Lovenia Descent to Upper East Fork Blacks Fork

To	Miles	Gain/Loss	Time Est.	Class
Upper East Fork camping area (M7.1)	3.8	-2,695'/+325'	2.5 hrs	3

To Red Knob Pass: 1.5 miles, -1,380'/+325', 1.5 hrs

This is the final part of the Lovenia Loop that started from upper East Fork Blacks Fork (M7.1). From the summit of Lovenia, you'll descend northwest to Red Knob Pass and then walk down the trail.

The route is quite rough and has some cliff bands of various sizes, but you can scramble down them or bypass them to the left (west) on loose slopes.

When you get near a large pillar (M7.8), descend the first wide break or gully you see to the left (west). Continue descending for a few minutes to steer clear of residual cliff bands, and then head back to the ridge. This route is described in more details as an *ascent* in the "Mount Lovenia, from Red Knob Pass" description below.

Mount Lovenia, from Red Knob Pass
One-way Route Summary

Reference	Miles	Gain/Loss	Time Est.	Class
Map 7, P10	1.5	+1,380/-325	1.5-2 hrs	3

The route begins at Red Knob Pass (M7.10 and M6.2), and goes up Lovenia's northwest ridge. From the top of Red Knob Pass, you can examine the entire ridge. There's never a dull moment on this continuously rough route. The only "relief" is the last ten to fifteen minutes to the top. You'll notice that the north-northwestern face of Lovenia is a massive system of cliff strata. These cliffs more or less end at the ridge top, but they're still the cause of some rough ground. The route bypasses the big cliffy areas by swinging out onto the southwestern slopes, which tend to be steep and loose with laborious climbing.

From the trail on Red Knob Pass, you'll have to descend southeast along a gentle Class 1 ridge top to a saddle (M7.9) before you can actually start climbing Lovenia. There are some very interesting rocks on this saddle, and a profusion of yellow flowers dots the slopes the first half of summer.

The relatively smooth saddle continues up Lovenia's ridge for a short distance, but within five minutes or so the "fun" begins. You'll encounter increasing roughness, with a few very small, broken rock bands (CL 2 or 2+). You'll shortly run into the largest cliffs of the route (M7.8), a conglomeration of rugged cliff bands that includes a tall, thick pillar of rock situated on the ridge. Measured from its base (which is generally out of view on the eastern face), it's probably about seventy to one hundred feet high. You can bypass this clifflike area entirely by traversing beneath the cliffs and climbing back to the ridge on loose slopes. Or you can climb up through one of several breaks. The second break or gully you come to is a good choice. This break has short cliff walls on both sides, and contains piles of loose talus rock you can pick your way up (CL 2+ or 3).

Either way, make your way back to the ridge top, where you'll climb up rough rock (CL 2+ or 3) to a bulky, broad abutment that creates a high point and minisaddle, at USGS elevation point 12531, about the midpoint of the

Mount Lovenia's northwest ridge, view from Red Knob Pass

climb. Traverse beneath the abutment and its associated ten- to thirty-foot cliff, and get back on the ridge.

Staying near the ridge top, you'll continue steady climbing up Class 2 to 2+ rough boulders, eventually reaching another high point or knoll, which you can scramble around or swing out wider onto loose slopes. From there, the ridge averages Class 2 climbing, with a few more minor rock bands, followed by the final, much lower-angled ridge and easy terrain to the summit.

GROUP 2: Red Castle Area Summits

- Mount Powell: 13,159 feet (#14)
- Wilson Peak: 13,055 feet (#19)

The two peaks in this Group are situated on the Uinta crest, on either side of Red Castle Peak. The Red Castle area is a popular basin. Red Castle Peak is perhaps the most recognizable and marvelous mountain formation in the Uintas, and is surrounded by large, beautiful lakes. If you can, I'd recommend adding some time to your peak-climbing trip to explore the basin, which is also a moose haven. One late September trip, I was lucky enough to see two huge bull moose in battle, clashing antlers in a meadow above Lower Red Castle Lake, with a couple of cow moose watching.

Although the trailside views are great, I think the best way to appreciate the grandeur of this area is to see it from the top of the surrounding high peaks. And the view doesn't get any better than from Wilson Peak and Mount Powell. Mount Powell is unique because it has three distinct high points in close proximity. Mount Wilson has a distinctive summit ridge that is narrow and almost flat for two-thirds of a mile, best seen from Red Castle Lake.

The East Fork Smiths Fork Trail (see Map 8), starting at the China Meadows Trailhead, has the most scenic Red Castle views, but an alternative approach trail is the Yellowstone Creek Trail (see Map 13) starting from the south at the Swift Creek Trailhead. The Yellowstone Creek Trail is described in Group 3 (see page 102) because it's commonly used to climb Kings Peak. Both trails have fairly easy walking (a gradual grade), but to reach Smiths Fork Pass, the Yellowstone Creek Trail is four miles longer and gains eighteen hundred more feet.

Both Wilson (see Map 9) and Powell (see Map 10) are conveniently accessed from Smiths Fork Pass. The two summits can be climbed on the same day if you camp strategically. Keep in mind that the terrain for two to three miles on either side of Smiths Fork Pass is above timberline and exposed to thunderstorms. Another option would be to take a couple of days for the scenic tour, climbing Wilson's northwest ridge from Red Castle Lake, and Powell from Smiths Fork Pass.

Estimated Time for an All-Inclusive Trip: three to four days (not including rest days, bad weather days, or driving time)

Trailhead Information

Driving directions, parking and campground information are detailed in the "Driving to the Trailheads" section. To drive to the China Meadows Trailhead (East Fork Smiths Fork Trail), see "North Slope Trailheads from I-80" on page 39. To drive to the Swift Creek Trailhead (Yellowstone Creek Trail), see page 48.

Trail and Round-Trip Route Summaries

East Fork Smiths Fork Trail (Map 8)

TRAILHEAD: China Meadows, Elev. 9,470′
TIME ESTIMATE: 7.5 hrs to Smiths Fork Pass, 6.5 hrs to Red Castle Lake

Destination (one-way)	Miles	Elevation	Elev. Gain
Upper-basin camping area (M8.8)	10.5	10,960′	+1,490′
Smiths Fork Pass (M8.9)	12.8	11,800′	+2,330′
Red Castle Lake (M8.10)	11.4	11,295′	+1,825′

Yellowstone Creek Trail (Maps 13 and 8)

TRAILHEAD: Swift Creek, Elev. 8,115′
TIME ESTIMATE: 9.5 hrs to upper-basin camping area, 10.5 hrs to Smiths Fork Pass

Destination (one-way)	Miles	Elevation	Elev. Gain
Upper-basin camping area (M8.19, M13.7)	15.4	11,000′	+2,885′
Smiths Fork Pass (M8.9)	16.7	11,800′	+3,685′

Round-Trip Routes

Peaks: Starting Points	Elev. Gain	Miles	Time Est.	Grade
Wilson Peak (Map 9)				
Smiths Fork Pass (M9.3)	+1,255′	2.4	2.5 hrs	I
Upper Smiths Fork camping area (M9.2)	+2,095′	7.0	4.5 hrs	II
Red Castle Lake (M9.5)	+1,760′	5.2	4.5 hrs	II
Upper Yellowstone camping area (M10.6)	+2,055′	6.2	4 hrs	II
TRAILHEAD (China Meadows—M8)	+3,585′	28.0	—	—
TRAILHEAD (Swift Creek–Yellowstone—M13)	+4,940′	35.8	—	—

Starting Point	Elev. Gain	Miles	Time Est.	Grade
Mount Powell (Map 10)				
Smiths Fork Pass (M10.1)	+2,020'	5.1	4 hrs	II
Upper Smiths Fork camping area (M9.2)	+2,860'	9.5	6 hrs	III
Upper Yellowstone camping area (M10.6)	+2,495'	5.8	4.5 hrs	II
TRAILHEAD (China Meadows—M8)	+4,350'	30.7	—	—
TRAILHEAD (Swift Creek—M13)	+5,380'	36.6	—	—
Wilson, Powell (Maps 9, 10)				
Smiths Fork Pass (M9.3, M10.1)	+3,275'	7.5	6.5 hrs	III
Upper Smiths Fork camping area (M9.2)	+4,115'	12.1	8.5 hrs	IV
Upper Yellowstone camping area (M10.6)	+3,875'	9.6	7.5 hrs	IV
TRAILHEAD (China Meadows—M8)	+5,605'	33.1	—	—
TRAILHEAD (Swift Creek—M13)	+7,840'	40.5	—	—

East Fork Smiths Fork Trail

Map point	M8.1	M8.2	M8.4	M8.5	M8.7	M8.8	M8.9	M8.10
Miles from trailhead	1.5	3.5	6.0	7.3	8.6	10.5	12.8	11.4

The East Fork Smiths Fork Trail (#110 on Forest Service maps) starts from the China Meadows Trailhead and ends at Red Castle Lake (M8.10). Another trail (#111) branches off just before Lower Red Castle Lake and goes over Smiths Fork Pass (M8.9). Like most north-slope trails, good campsites are very abundant along the trail. As you'll discover, this trail also has a very well developed system of bridges and boardwalks.

The trail starts at a gate near a large trailhead billboard. A separate horse trail coming from farther back in the campground joins in shortly.

You'll be hiking through a mixed forest for the first part of the trail. Just shy of a mile from the trailhead you'll enter the official wilderness area, marked by a sign. After going through a couple of dry meadows, you'll cross the East Fork (M8.1) on a very sturdy bridge. For the next mile and a half after the bridge, the trail is just inside the timber, running next to a long meadow with willow clusters and a stream, a likely moose hangout.

Shortly after a *very* long boardwalk, you'll pass through a gated fence, and five to ten minutes later, you'll reach a trail junction (M8.2). The trail to Lake Hessie, a part of the North Slope Highline Trail, angles back to the left. Continue straight ahead (you might actually pass by the Lake Hessie Trail without realizing it, as the junction isn't marked well). A half mile later there's yet another trail junction (M8.3), marked by a huge sign nailed to a tree. Here the North Slope Highline Trail leaves and goes west downslope. Continue straight ahead.

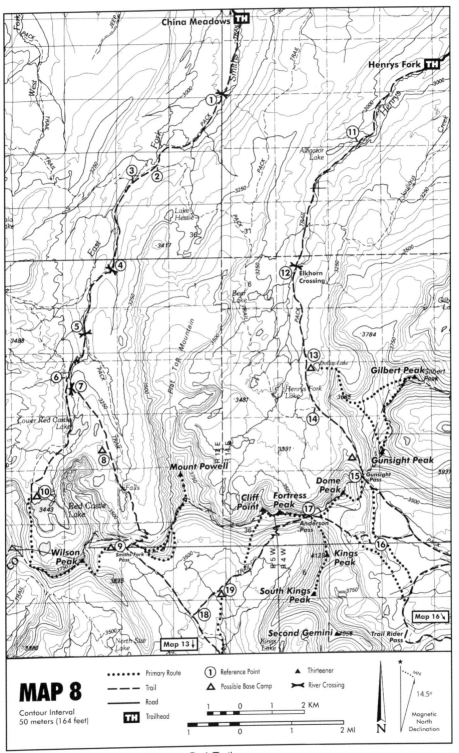

China Meadows TH
Henrys Fork TH

① ③ ② ④ ⑤ ⑥ ⑦ ⑧ ⑨ ⑩ ⑪ ⑫ Elkhorn Crossing ⑬ ⑭ ⑮ ⑯ ⑰ ⑱ ⑲

Alligator Lake
Lake Hessie
Bear Lake
Henrys Fork Lake
Dollar Lake
Gilbert Peak
Gunsight Peak
Gunsight Pass
Dome Peak
Fortress Peak
Cliff Point
Anderson Pass
Mount Powell
Lower Red Castle Lake
Falls
Red Castle Lake
Wilson Peak
Smiths Fork Pass
Kings Peak
South Kings Peak
Second Gemini
Kings Lake
North Star Lake
Trail Rider Pass
West Fork
East Fork
Flat Top Mountain

Map 13 ↓
Map 16 ↘

MAP 8

Contour Interval
50 meters (164 feet)

•••••• Primary Route
– – – Trail
——— Road
TH Trailhead

① Reference Point
△ Possible Base Camp

▲ Thirteener
✕ River Crossing

Magnetic North Declination
14.5°
N

East Fork Smiths Fork Trail and Henrys Fork Trail

About two miles later you'll cross a larger tributary to the East Fork (M8.4). The trail crosses this nice-size stream in several places over logs (hey, what happened to the bridges, the boardwalks?).

After cutting back to the west, the trail reaches the enormous Broadbent Meadow, a half mile from the last stream crossing. From here, on the right-hand skyline, there's a nice view of the rather nifty-looking red rounded ridges of Bald Mountain.

Leaving Broadbent Meadow, you'll eventually come to another bridge (M8.5) spanning the East Fork, where Red Castle Peak suddenly

View of Red Castle and Tokewanna Peak (left skyline) from Mount Powell

bursts into view, standing dramatically in the upper basin. Just after the bridge you can also see Mount Powell on the skyline to your left, with its distinctive three-humped summit. (Note that USGS topographic maps show a trail continuing up the drainage *before* crossing the bridge, but it is no longer used and has faded from view.)

A short distance up the trail after crossing the bridge, the river (mostly obscured by trees) empties down into a gorge as it leaves the upper-basin meadows below Lower Red Castle Lake. In a series of six switchbacks, you'll gain elevation quickly as the trail climbs high above the river gorge. The forest makeup changes as you climb—transitioning from lodgepoles at the bottom to a mostly Engelmann spruce forest at the top.

Shortly after topping out, you'll leave the timber and enter a large meadow, where the basin opens up into a sweeping Red Castle panorama. There's a trail junction here (M8.6), adjacent to where the river tumbles over some bedrock. The Bald Mountain Trail goes back to the right. Continue straight ahead.

A few minutes later you'll reach an important trail junction (M8.7 and M9.1). If you're going the Smiths Fork Pass route to Wilson and Powell, take the East Red Castle Trail going left (east). The trail to the right (straight ahead) goes past Lower Red Castle Lake and ends at Red Castle Lake, where the "Wilson Peak, from Red Castle Lake" route begins.

At the time of this writing, there were permanent fire closures (no fires or wood gathering) within one thousand feet of Lower Red Castle Lake or the smaller unnamed lake just to the east of it.

To Smiths Fork Pass (M8.9 and M9.3) from the Trail Junction (M8.7 and M9.1): 3.9 miles, +1,080 feet

Going left (east) on the East Red Castle Trail, you'll immediately cross the East Fork on a sturdy plank bridge with no side rails. The trail goes through some small, pretty meadows, then starts climbing more steadily over forested and rocky hills. The timber obscures most views of the peaks. Most maps seem to be inaccurate or out of date through this section (see Map 8 or 9 for my approximation).

About a mile and a half after the trail junction, the trail passes through a great camping area with a small side stream nearby running through a meadow (M8.8 and M9.2). This is about as high as you can go and still find good camping below timberline with convenient water.

Route Segment	Miles	Gain/Loss	Time Est.
Camping area (M9.2) to Smiths Fork Pass (M9.3)	2.3	+840	1-1.5 hrs

Eventually, you'll leave the forest and pop out into the high open country beneath Smiths Fork Pass. This upper-basin or plateau area is all above timberline and very scenic. To your left in the river valley, a couple of waterfalls cascade down the bedrock. Mount Powell looms above you directly to the east.

Going farther up into the basin, you'll pass by the high-altitude, tree-barren Smiths Fork Pass Lake. Smiths Fork Pass itself is a fairly gentle climb, but it's deceptively long.

About one-third of a mile to the west from the top of the pass, there's a little lake (M8.9 and M9.3). It's a possibility for a base camp—however, the lake water is a bit stale, and the surrounding terrain is very rocky and openly exposed to the elements.

To Red Castle Lake (M8.10 and M9.5) from the Trail Junction (M8.7 and M9.1): 2.5 miles, +575 feet

The trail initially traces the right (west) side of the large meadow. It passes above Lower Red Castle Lake, and soon enters the timber. Climbing steadily for close to a mile, the trail eventually breaks out of the trees and climbs up through a cliff band. You'll top out on the large, flat plateau where Red Castle Lake sits. From here there's a fantastic view of the very broad, precipitous north face of Wilson Peak, the summit being the high knoll on the far left side of the flat-looking ridge top.

This area is quite exposed, but you could camp almost anywhere in the flats north of Red Castle Lake, and in a few places on the west side along the route to Wilson Peak. There are also good off-trail possibilities near timberline to the northwest, before (beneath) the Red Castle plateau.

Wilson Peak, from Smiths Fork Pass
One-way Route Summary

Reference	Miles	Gain/Loss	Time Est.	Class
Map 9, P3	1.2	+1,255′	1.5 hrs	3

This route goes west from Smiths Fork Pass, climbs five hundred feet up to the saddle (M9.4) southeast of Wilson Peak, then follows the ridge to the summit. Looking at the route, you'll notice a section of red rock bands directly beneath the saddle. The rock bands are residual cliffs that extend out from Wilson's eastern face. The route skirts these rock layers to the left (south), and then angles up to the saddle.

From Smiths Fork Pass, begin hiking west across the bouldered, grassy slopes (CL 1). This area has easy walking and is very scenic, with sweeping views down into the Yellowstone drainage. You'll be walking to the point where the southeastern slopes of Wilson converge with the northern slopes of Peak 12779 to the south.

Climbing up the slope toward the saddle, you'll at first go through stable sections (CL 1+) with patchy grass. The slope gradually transitions to harder terrain. As you climb, aim for the dark gray-green rock layer, which sits just to the left of the top of the saddle.

Above the midway point, the slope gets more and more loose, and considerably steeper—Class 3 climbing due to the looseness of the soil and rock and having to work through small rock bands. You can console yourself with the fact that this slope is an easy and very fast descent.

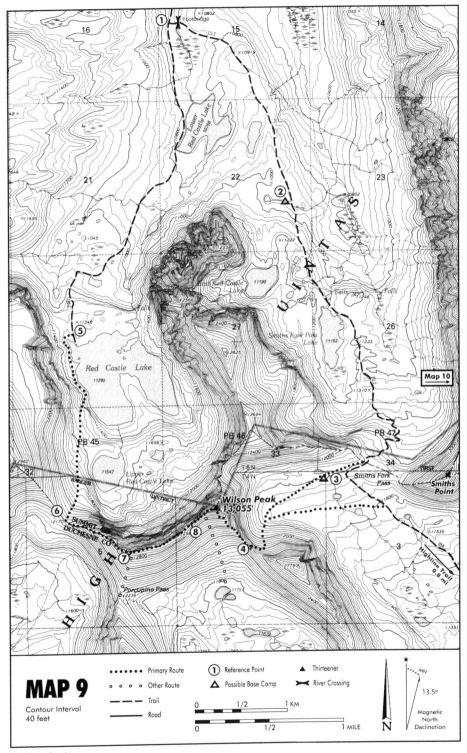

MAP 9

Contour Interval
40 feet

.... Primary Route
○ ○ ○ ○ Other Route
– – – Trail
——— Road

① Reference Point
△ Possible Base Camp

▲ Thirteener
⋈ River Crossing

0   1/2   1 KM

0   1/2   1 MILE

N

MN

13.5°

Magnetic
North
Declination

Wilson Peak

The last seventy-five vertical feet (or so) to the saddle are the toughest. Unless you go off route and end up climbing a more direct route through the cliff bands, danger is minimal (rocks knocked loose by climbing partners are the main hazard on this route).

When you've almost reached the top of the saddle, you'll see above you a transition area where red rock meets dark gray-green rock. It's tempting to climb directly up through these rock bands to the top, and skip the loose stuff, but it turns out to be a short Class 4+ climb on crumbly shale. A better route is an ascending traverse, starting about fifteen vertical feet below and about eighty feet away from the low point of the saddle. At this point you can make a straight-across traverse on a sloping, loose shelf immediately below the dark rock band and just above the highest red rock band.

The saddle is patterned with colorful, layered, platelike rocks with geometric shapes. They're no match for the rocks atop Mount Powell, but interesting nonetheless.

The rest of the route to the summit along the ridge top alternates Class 2 and 3 sections. The last three to five minutes get rougher—if you stick to the ridge crest, it turns into a Class 3+ scramble, but going even a short distance to the west, away from the ridge, makes it easier (CL 2 or 2+).

The perspective of Red Castle Peak and Red Castle Lake from the summit makes the climb well worth the effort. This particular route to Wilson is great because most of the scene is hidden until reaching the very top, where it suddenly appears in all its glory.

Wilson Peak, from Upper Yellowstone
One-way Route Summary

Reference	Miles	Gain/Loss	Time Est.	Class
Maps 9 and 10 (M10.6)	3.1	+2,055′	2-2.5 hrs	3

This route starts from the upper Yellowstone base-camping area (M10.6) by the Highline Trail. You simply follow the Highline Trail back to the Smiths Fork Trail junction, and walk up-trail (north) toward Smiths Fork Pass. It's easy to go cross-country around here, so you can shortcut across the meadows as you see fit. Before reaching the top of Smiths Fork Pass, leave the trail and hike across very easy slopes and rocky meadows to the base of Wilson Peak. The rest of the route is explained in the "Wilson Peak, from Smiths Fork Pass" description above.

Wilson Peak's flat-topped summit ridge

Wilson Peak, from Red Castle Lake

One-way Route Summary

Reference	Miles	Gain/Loss	Time Est.	Class
Map 9, P5	2.6	+1,760	2.5 hrs	3

From Red Castle Lake, this route goes to the pass (M9.6) northwest of Wilson Peak, scrambles up the ridge, then follows Wilson's long, mostly flat summit ridge to the high point.

From the northwestern corner of Red Castle Lake, contour around the western shores (CL 1). There's a faint trail with occasional cairns that goes through the boulders and patchy vegetation at the base of Squaw Peak's talus slopes. In about a half mile you'll reach a vegetated, rocky bluff rising directly above the lake waters. Steer to the right and climb on top of the bluff. From here, make a long, gradually ascending traverse of the cirque's west side. You'll be following a sloped, grassy shelf (CL 1 to 1+) that conveniently leads to the top of the pass (M9.6). The pass is the approximate halfway point for both distance and elevation.

The ridgeline from the pass to the beginning of the flat-topped summit ridge (at M9.7) may appear intimidating. But it's more doable than it looks—you can bypass the cliffs, making it no harder than Class 2+, although the loose slopes away from the ridge crest do get tiresome.

Approximately fifteen minutes up from the pass you'll come to a thirty-foot-high cliff band. You can handily get around it by traversing beneath it to the right (the west face). Go about eighty feet and you'll see a couple of short rock climbs up the cliff, in the Class 4+ to 5 range. However, if you continue the traverse for another hundred feet or so, the cliff band breaks up completely. Either way, climb back up to the ridge crest.

Shortly thereafter (in maybe ten minutes), you'll encounter another cliff band of a similar nature. Just barely to the right of the ridge crest, there's a Class 3+ ten- to fifteen-foot scramble up the cliff. Or traverse beneath it to the right (the west face) for a couple of minutes and you'll find several less difficult ways up (CL 2). Again, make your way back up to the ridge top.

Nearing the top, you'll scramble through a rugged section characterized by small rock bands (CL 2+ to 3, depending on your particular route). Zigzag around and through this rugged area, mostly on or just to the right of the ridge.

You'll eventually top out onto the westernmost point of Wilson's long, narrow summit ridge (M9.7). From here, the hike to the ridge's low point (M9.8) is a pleasurable, near-level, flat pathway (CL 1), almost as if someone had sheared off the top of the mountain. In fact, a few minutes from the western point, you'll reach a fascinating section where the rock is so flat it's a veritable sidewalk. You'll enjoy inspiring views as you go, beginning with a long-distance view down the Oweep Creek corridor to the west and the ever spectacular Red Castle landscape.

Approaching the low point near the summit, the north face becomes a sheer precipice, even overhanging at times, with rock slabs creating some large, narrow crevices on the ridge top (which can be easily bypassed). From the low point, the flat ridge comes to an end, and you can hop up typical Uinta boulders (CL 2) to the summit.

Mount Powell, from Smiths Fork Pass
One-way Route Summary

Reference	Miles	Gain/Loss	Time Est.	Class
Map 10, P1	2.7	+1,730'/-365'	2 hrs	2+ (3+)

This route goes east from Smiths Fork Pass and over (or around) Smiths Point (AN). You have two routes to choose from (see Map 10). Route A circles around Smiths Point through the meadows at the base. Route B goes over Smiths Point, traversing the face near the top. The routes converge at Powell Saddle (AN) and follow Powell's southwest ridge to the summit. Route A is

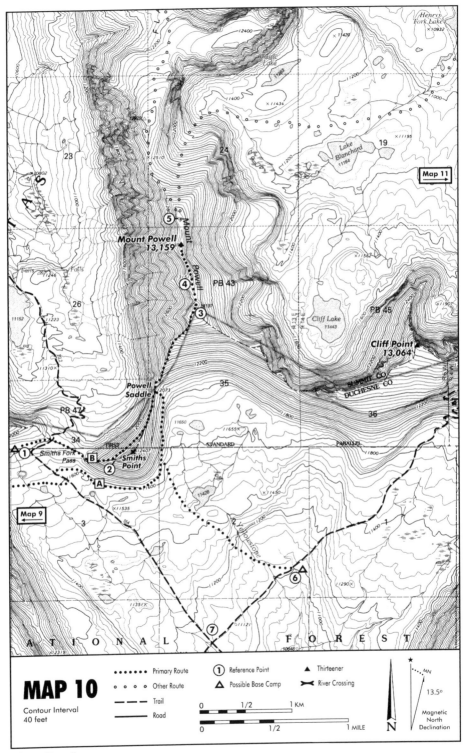

Mount Powell

about one-third of a mile longer than Route B, but is easier. The two routes have roughly the same overall elevation gain and loss.

ROUTE A: THE BASE OF SMITHS POINT, CLASS 1+

From Smiths Fork Pass, it's an easy descent on gently rolling moraine slopes with a few boulder patches. The hiking is fast, and you'll soon round the southeast corner of Smiths Point, allowing a view of Powell and the basin beneath. A decaying, old cliff band circles around just above the basin meadows. You can pass through it in various places, but an

Mount Powell's ridge crest, view south from middle summit

easy route simply traverses above it. Walk toward the cliff band for about ten to fifteen minutes, then head upslope to your left in an ascending traverse. Above the cliff band, you can zigzag along easy grass shelves (CL 1 to 1+) and over boulder striations to Powell Saddle.

ROUTE B: OVER SMITHS POINT, CLASS 2+

From Smiths Fork Pass, walk east to the base of the Smiths Point ridge. There are some fascinating striped "tiger" boulders scattered around grassy slopes. Start hiking up the ridge. It's grassy with intermittent rocks anchored in, but surprisingly steep (CL 2). Normally, ridge tops are the routes of choice, but in this case the summit is a mess of chopped-up rock bands. The lower half of Smith Point's face is a cliffy slide area—particularly the area adjacent to Powell Saddle—so the best strategy is to climb well above the halfway point on the ridge, then do a traverse. A good place to start the traverse is at a greenish soil layer just beyond where the vegetation and grass end (M10.2). It'll be slow going Class 2+ on arduous, shifty boulders. At the end of the traverse, go down Smith Point's northeast ridge (CL 2). You'll go over a fun series of terraces with short three- to five-foot drops and end up at Powell Saddle.

From Powell Saddle, simply continue up Mount Powell's southwest ridge. This ridge is an easy Class 2 for most of the way. Just before the top, you'll pass through a brief rough Class 3 section, maybe 3+ if you're directly on the ridge crest. It ends suddenly at the edge of a short, gently rounded slope leading to the south summit (M10.3) at 13,137 feet. Powell's highest point is the north summit (M10.5), about a half mile to the north. The ups and downs along the ridge crest are minor, but add up to several hundred more feet in elevation gain going to the north summit and back.

Going north along the ridge from the south summit, you'll go over a brief rough section, and then have a very easy walk to the middle summit (M10.4) at 13,151 feet. At the low point between the south and middle summits, there's a fascinating part of the ridge top that looks like angular cobblestones, almost as if someone carefully placed rectangular rocks tightly together.

The smooth sailing you might have expected of rounded-looking Powell soon comes to an end—you'll have to pass through some cliff bands before reaching the north summit.

Hiking north off the middle summit, there's a cliff band that you'll go down in two stages. First, staying near the ridge crest, climb down a five-foot Class 3+ drop. Then walk about thirty to fifty feet back to the south on the west (left-hand) face, where you can down-climb through the second rock band (CL 3 or easier). There are probably several places you could get down.

The ridge gets flat again, and a couple of minutes later, you'll reach another cliff band. The easiest way to get down this cliff is to stay on the crest. You'll go down a short five-foot drop (CL 4), then a slightly easier ten-foot section (CL 3+).

This brings you to the low point just before the north summit, where it's an easy walk to the top. Like Wilson Peak, Mount Powell offers an opportunity to see Red Castle from above. From this vantage point, East Red Castle Lake is especially beautiful, nestled beneath the red crags. In addition to other 13ers, you'll also have a nice head-on view of Kings Peak and its western face. If you're trying to reach all twenty-five *points* above thirteen thousand feet (versus the twenty-one peaks), then continue to the spur (M10.5) less than one-fifth of a mile away.

Mount Powell, from Upper Yellowstone
One-way Route Summary

Reference	Miles	Gain/Loss	Time Est.	Class
Map 10, P6	2.9	+2,330'/-165'	2-2.5 hrs	2+ (3+)

From the upper Yellowstone area, you can take a more direct route to Mount Powell, without having to negotiate Smiths Point like you do from Smiths Fork Pass. The route goes north from the Highline Trail and connects to the route from Smiths Fork Pass, which goes up to Powell Saddle. Refer to "Mount Powell, from Smiths Fork Pass" for details. There's a minor rocky area around Yellowstone Creek just above the Highline Trail, but otherwise the route has all easy slopes and grassy meadows. You could also go directly up Powell's south face instead of going to Powell Saddle. It's more bouldered and a bit steeper but still doable.

GROUP 3: Kings Peak Area Summits

- Kings Peak: 13,528 feet (#1)
- South Kings Peak: 13,512 feet (#2)
- Gilbert Peak: 13,442 feet (#3)
- Gunsight Peak (AN): 13,263 feet (#8)
- Fortress Peak (AN): 13,260 feet (#9)
- Dome Peak (AN): 13,103 feet (#16)
- Cliff Point (AN): 13,064 feet (#18)

This Group includes the three highest peaks in Utah—Kings Peak, South Kings Peak, and Gilbert Peak—as well as four other 13ers. Kings Peak and South Kings Peak, the first and second highest peaks in Utah, were named after Clarence King, a pioneer geologist of the Uintas.

Using the Henrys Fork Trail (see Map 8), you can access any Group 3 summit. The Henrys Fork basin is spacious in comparison to other north-slope basins. It's very picturesque, especially the Uinta crest at the head of the basin. In late-evening light, the area looks like a muted, subtle painting, accented by multicolored talus and rock layers. Every main high point at the head or side of the upper Henrys Fork basin is a 13er. Fortress Peak, sitting at the center of the basin, is especially impressive with its magnificent, sheer north face and classic mountain profile. You can also see pyramid-shaped Kings Peak rising above a notch between Dome Peak and Fortress Peak.

The Henrys Fork Trail is the most popular trail in the Uintas, visited by thousands of hikers and horse packers every year. The majority of the hikers going into the Henrys Fork basin are headed for Kings Peak and use Dollar Lake or Henrys Fork Lake for a base camp, so camp elsewhere to avoid the crowds. In fact, the Forest Service has placed a permanent ban on campfires and wood gathering within one thousand feet of those two lakes. The Forest Service has posted the following: "Use and impact in Henrys Fork Basin has steadily increased. Much of the dead wood is gone, campers are cutting green trees, and campfires have blackened the soil in some areas. Increasing numbers of campers will more than likely require us to expand the fire closure in the future." But don't let all this discourage your visit. Henrys Fork is still a gorgeous wilderness-quality area—just heavily used.

Another way to access some Group 3 summits is the long, beautifully forested Yellowstone Creek Trail (see Map 13), which starts at the Swift Creek Trailhead on the south side of the Uintas. It starts about thirteen hundred feet lower than the Henrys Fork Trail and is five and one-half miles longer to Anderson Pass. From Yellowstone you can also climb both Wilson and Powell in Group 2. For a more extended trip, you could even try the Atwood Basin Trail (see Maps 8 and 14), and climb Group 4 summits along the way to Group 3.

It should come as no surprise that Kings Peak, Utah's high point, sees a lot of traffic. On heavy weekends, Forest Service rangers have counted 150-200 people heading for the summit. So it is likely you'll be sharing the top with another party. However, you can avoid the biggest crowds and possibly have the summit to yourself by going midweek instead of on holidays or weekends (Sunday night often finds the trailhead parking lot almost deserted) or early or late season.

Climbing Kings Peak and surrounding 13ers (see Map 12) is almost too easy, thanks to the Highline Trail over Anderson Pass—the highest trail in the Uintas—and the adjoining trail from Gunsight Pass. It also helps that Fortress and Cliff Point are so close together. From a base camp in either the Henrys Fork or Yellowstone basin, strong hikers can climb all five peaks (Kings, South Kings, Dome, Fortress, and Cliff Point) in one long, spectacular day. Such a feat is easier from Yellowstone, because you can insert a loop into the route by descending south of Cliff Point, plus Yellowstone's traditional base-camping area is closer to the summits. Of course, there's no need to rush things—a more leisurely grouping strategy is to climb Kings and South Kings together, and on another day do Dome, Fortress, and Cliff Point.

Gilbert and Gunsight are best climbed from Henrys Fork via Dollar Lake (see Map 11), arguably the all-around easiest route to both summits. The relatively short Henrys Fork Trail makes an overnight or quick weekend trip to Gilbert, Gunsight, Kings Peak, or other Group 3 summits very doable.

Estimated Time for an All-Inclusive Trip: four to five days (not including rest days, bad weather days, or driving time)

Trailhead Information

Driving directions, parking and campground information are detailed in the "Driving to the Trailheads" section. You can drive to the Henrys Fork Trailhead from either I-80 in Wyoming (see page 39) or from the town of Lonetree,

Wyoming (see page 46). To drive to the Swift Creek Trailhead (Yellowstone Creek Trail), see page 48.

Trail and Round-Trip Route Summaries

Henrys Fork Trail (Map 8)

TRAILHEAD: Henrys Fork, Elev. 9,430'
TIME ESTIMATE: 4 hrs to Dollar Lake

Destination (one-way)	Miles	Elevation	Elev. Gain
Dollar Lake (M8.13)	7.2	10,785'	+1,355'
Gunsight Pass (M8.15)	10.0	11,888'	+2,460'
Anderson Pass* (M8.17)	11.5	12,690'	+3,260'

*Via Gunsight Cutoff

Yellowstone Creek Trail (Maps 13 and 8)

TRAILHEAD: Swift Creek, Elev. 8,115'
TIME ESTIMATE: 9.5 hrs to upper-basin camping area

Destination (one-way)	Miles	Elevation	Elev. Gain
Upper-basin camping area (M8.19, M13.7)	15.4	11,000'	+3,005'/-120'
Anderson Pass (M8.17)	18.2	12,690'	+4,695'/-120'

Round-Trip Routes

Peaks: Starting Points	Elev. Gain	Miles	Time Est.	Grade
Gilbert, Gunsight (Map 11)				
Dollar Lake (M11.1)	+3,295'	7.3	5.5 hrs	III
TRAILHEAD (Henrys Fork—M8)	+4,650'	21.7	—	—
Gilbert Peak (Map 11)				
Dollar Lake (M11.1)	+2,655'	5.6	4 hrs	II
TRAILHEAD (Henrys Fork—M8)	+4,010'	20.0	—	—
Gunsight Peak (Map 11)				
Dollar Lake (M11.1)	+2,480'	5.4	3.5 hrs	II
TRAILHEAD (Henrys Fork—M8)	+3,835'	19.8	—	—
Dome Peak (Maps 11, 12)				
Dollar Lake (M11.1)	+2,320'	7.2	5 hrs	II
TRAILHEAD (Henrys Fork—M8)	+3,675'	21.6	—	—
Kings Peak (Map 12)				
Dollar Lake (M11.1)	+2,745'	10.0	6.5 hrs	III
Upper Yellowstone camping area (M12.13)	+2,530'	7.0	4 hrs	II
TRAILHEAD (Henrys Fork—M8)	+4,100'	24.4	—	—
TRAILHEAD (Swift Creek—M13)	+5,655'	37.8	—	—

Peaks: Starting Points	Elev. Gain	Miles	Time Est.	Grade
Kings, South Kings (Map 12)				
Dollar Lake (M11.1)	+3,630'	11.6	8 hrs	IV
Upper Yellowstone camping area (M12.13)	+3,415'	8.6	5.5 hrs	III
TRAILHEAD (Henrys Fork—M8)	+4,985'	26.0	—	—
TRAILHEAD (Swift Creek—M13)	+6,540'	39.4	—	—
Fortress, Cliff Point (Map 12)				
Dollar Lake (M11.1)	+2,740'	10.8	6.5 hrs	III
Upper Yellowstone camping area (M12.13)	+2,295'	5.7	3.5 hrs	II
TRAILHEAD (Henrys Fork—M8)	+4,095'	25.2	—	—
TRAILHEAD (Swift Creek—M13)	+5,420'	36.5	—	—
Dome, Fortress, Cliff Point (Map 12)				
Dollar Lake (M11.1)	+3,405'	10.9	7 hrs	IV
Upper Yellowstone camping area (M12.13)	+3,210'	7.3	5 hrs	III
TRAILHEAD (Henrys Fork—M8)	+4,760'	25.3	—	—
TRAILHEAD (Swift Creek—M13)	+6,335'	38.1	—	—
Kings, South Kings, Dome, Fortress, Cliff Point (Map 12)				
Dollar Lake (M11.1)	+5,130'	13.9	10 hrs	V
Upper Yellowstone camping area (M12.13)	+4,935'	10.3	8 hrs	IV
TRAILHEAD (Henrys Fork—M8)	+6,485'	28.3	—	—
TRAILHEAD (Swift Creek—M13)	+8,060'	41.1	—	—

All routes to Anderson Pass from Henrys Fork use the Gunsight Cutoff

Henrys Fork Trail

Map point	M8.11	M8.12	M8.13	M8.14	M8.15	M8.16	M8.17
Miles from trailhead	2.3	5.2	7.2	8.0	10.0	11.0	12.8

The Henrys Fork Trail (#117 on Forest Service maps) is easy to follow and has a steady, gentle grade all the way to Gunsight Pass (M8.15), making it a fast trail to hike. It also has a lot of board walkways and footbridges. From Gunsight Pass, you can connect to the Highline Trail using either the Highline Shortcut (AN) or the Gunsight Cutoff (AN). The Highline Trail climbs to Anderson Pass (M8.17), a takeoff point for five of the 13ers in this Group.

The trail begins at the far end of the parking lot at a trail register. For the first couple of miles you're well above the river, separated by steep slopes or a rocky gorge. You'll be walking through a mixed forest of evergreens and aspens.

In just over two miles from the trailhead, you'll reach the trail junction (M8.11) with Alligator Lake. The next couple of miles from Alligator Lake you'll find several decent campsites near water. The canyon below the Alligator Lake trail junction narrows significantly as the river goes through a small but scenic, rocky gorge. As you walk through intermittent small meadows, you'll have views of Gilbert's southern ridge to your left, now above timberline. Gilbert Peak itself is still hidden.

About five miles from the trailhead you'll reach a major trail junction, called Elkhorn Crossing (M8.12). The trail splits, allowing horses and hikers to cross separately. Hikers take the left-hand spur, which drops immediately down to the river and crosses on a footbridge composed of four sturdy logs. There are many attractive campsites within shaded forest just after the crossing, the best camping along the entire trail (before the upper basin).

Immediately after the campsite cluster, you'll reach the junction with the North Slope Highline Trail, marked by a sign. Some topographic maps show this trail joining earlier (lower down), but that junction apparently no longer exists or isn't obvious.

The trail enters a long, rocky meadow, filled with low-growth willow shrubs. This meadow is the beginning of the upper-basin open country and has the first of many views of the high peaks, including Mount Powell and Fortress Peak.

About half a mile from Elkhorn Crossing, the trail leaves the river bottoms and starts going more steeply uphill. You'll top out in meadows on the basin's east bench, just a mile and a half away from Dollar Lake. The east bench has superb views of all the 13ers in this basin, as well as a nice view of the route to Gilbert that follows the ridge above Dollar Lake. Gilbert Peak is the square-looking summit on the left-hand skyline. Kings Peak is the triangular-shaped peak seen through a notch in the middle of the basin's headwall.

After walking on the scenic east bench for about one and one-half miles, you'll cross a good-size side stream, and five minutes later you'll enter a (brief) forested area with decent campsites (M8.13). Dollar Lake is less than a quarter mile off the trail to your left (east). If you're looking, you can see it through the forest, but you won't see a sign or distinct trail leading to it. The Dollar Lake area is pretty much the last below-timberline camping area you'll find on the Henrys Fork Trail.

Be doubly sure to purify water around here, as there is an enormous herd of sheep (I estimated at least six hundred on one of my Gilbert climbs) that hangs out in the drainage above Dollar Lake. The semiloop route to Gilbert Peak and Gunsight Peak begins on the eastern side of Dollar Lake (see page 106 and Map 11).

Route Segment	Miles	Gain/Loss	Time Est.
Dollar Lake to Gunsight Pass	2.8	+1,105'	1.5 hrs
Dollar Lake to Anderson Pass*	4.3	+1,905'	2.5 hrs

*Via the Gunsight Cutoff

About a mile up the trail beyond Dollar Lake, you'll reach the junction with the Henrys Fork basin trail (M8.14 and M11.3), which takes a scenic, roundabout tour of the basin, going by Henrys Fork Lake, Island Lake, and Bear Lake, and joining the trail to Lake Hessie and East Fork Smiths Fork. If you're taking this detour, you'll probably have to walk across the grassy meadow to spot the faded trail.

Continuing southward up the trail, you'll reach the base of Gunsight Pass in about two miles. Because this general area (M11.4 and M12.1) is very close to the Kings-area summits, it is a tempting base camp. However, you'd be camping next to the trail and on fragile alpine vegetation, so if you must stay here it only makes sense for a quick overnighter. Water should be running at the base of the boulder field on the trail's west side. Also consider the small lake about five minutes downslope, which is arguably a better location. Both areas are of course above timberline.

Route Segment	Miles	Gain/Loss	Time Est.
Base of Gunsight Pass (M12.1) to Anderson Pass*	2.2	+1,210'	1.5 hrs

*Via the Gunsight Cutoff

The trail makes two very large, perfectly angled switchbacks to the top of Gunsight Pass, making quick work of the four-hundred-foot climb. To get to Kings Peak and other Group 3 summits from Gunsight Pass, I'd recommend using either the Highline Shortcut or the Gunsight Cutoff route rather than following the "official trail" (see Map 12 for details). The Gunsight Cutoff is the best (fastest) choice if you're out day hiking the peaks, but if you're backpacking to Anderson Pass, definitely take the Highline Shortcut.

GUNSIGHT CUTOFF TO ANDERSON PASS, FROM GUNSIGHT PASS: 1.5 MILES, +800 FEET

This route essentially climbs the first half of Dome Peak's eastern face. The route starts directly from the top of Gunsight Pass, leaving the official trail and making a traverse southwest. You'll probably see small cairns and a very faint path (worn into the mountainside through the years by other climbers). The route parallels the official trail below for a short distance, and then starts an ascending traverse of the slope (CL 1).

About ten to fifteen minutes from the pass, the trail starts steeply uphill and comes to a broken, short cliff band, where the path divides into two routes. The first route avoids the cliff band, traversing beneath it until it dies out, and then heads upslope. The second route goes directly up through the cliff band—a short Class 3 climb through the initial rock band, then standard Class 2 boulder climbing thereafter.

You'll top out (M12.5) on the edge of the large plateau that stretches between Gunsight Peak and Kings Peak (the plateau's cliffy eastern escarpment extends south for about three-quarters of a mile). Take note of where you come out, as on the way back the cairns can be camouflaged when you're looking down. From here, you can start climbing the slopes to Dome Peak (refer to the "Dome Peak, from Gunsight Pass" description), or walk across the rocky meadow (CL 1) to the Highline Trail going up to Anderson Pass.

HIGHLINE SHORTCUT TO ANDERSON PASS, FROM GUNSIGHT PASS: 2.8 MILES, −488/+1290 FEET

The Highline Shortcut isn't marked on maps, but a trail definitely exists (probably made from hikers or sheep or both), and it's easy. The "official" trail is a mile longer than the Highline Shortcut.

From the top of Gunsight Pass, descend southerly on the official trail. It makes a short switchback and then starts a long, descending traverse on a wide, vegetated terrace above some cliff bands. The traverse lasts about one-third of a mile, when the trail starts going down through a section of layered bedrock.

Around this rocky area (M12.2) the official trail drops immediately down to the basin flats. Stay on the Highline Shortcut by continuing your gradual traverse due south. The Highline Shortcut seems to be used more than the official trail, so chances are you'll miss the official trail and end up on the shortcut anyway.

The shortcut trail passes through a couple of small boulder fields, gradually reaching the flat meadows at the base of steep slopes coming off the Kings-Gunsight plateau. At the meadow's edge there's a small campsite area (M12.3 and M8.16) with a large spring nearby, gurgling out from beneath a boulder field. Stunted trees grow around here, but otherwise there's little cover.

From the small campsite, the trail starts going upslope again, but more steeply. A short distance after starting up, the trail fizzles out and cairns lead the rest of the way through rocks and shrubs up to the Highline Trail.

The Highline Trail makes several switchbacks before reaching the top of the sloping plateau. From here, you have an easy walk across the flats and a quick, moderate ascent to Anderson Pass (Map 12 and M8.17).

Note for the return trip along the Highline Shortcut: After descending halfway down from the plateau beneath Kings Peak, look for a flat area that contains a small, marshy off-trail pond (M12.4). This area is a signal to start heading due north downslope.

CAUTION: ANDERSON PASS VIA THE KINGS PEAK "SHORTCUT"

Between Anderson Knob (AN) (M12.10) and Dome Peak, you'll see a chute leading up to a notch in the ridge (M12.7). The route starts directly up from the small lake marked elevation point 11208. Other people have used it as a so-called shortcut, but the chute is actually very steep, unstable, and dangerous. The risk is not worth the amount of time saved (if any). Use Gunsight Cutoff instead.

TO GROUP 4 SUMMITS, FROM GUNSIGHT PASS

If you're backpacking to the Atwood Basin area over Trail Rider Pass, you'll save some time over the official trail by cutting across the gentle meadows in Painter Basin (see Maps 8 and 14 for an overview, Maps 12 and 16 for details). Take the Highline Shortcut down to the flats in Painter Basin. Contour at the base of the plateau and hills beneath Kings Peak, and then cut across toward Trail Rider Pass, catching the trail for the climb up to the top. You will essentially stay at the same elevation all the way to the base of Trail Rider Pass. You can eyeball the route before dropping down from Gunsight Pass. It's 3.8 miles from Gunsight Pass to Trail Rider Pass.

Yellowstone Creek Trail

Map point	M13.1	M13.2	M13.3	M13.4	M13.5	M13.6	M13.7	M8.17	M8.9
Miles from trailhead	3.3	5.0	8.8	11.0	13.7	14.7	15.4	18.2	16.7

The Yellowstone Creek Trail (#057 on Forest Service maps) starts at the Swift Creek Trailhead and follows Yellowstone Creek upstream. In the upper basin, it connects with the Highline Trail (M13.6 and M8.18), which goes northeast to Anderson Pass (M8.17) or northwest to Smiths Fork Pass (M8.9). The Yellowstone Creek Trail is the long way to get to Group 3 summits, but many people

Kings Peak (distant skyline), view from upper Yellowstone basin

still use it to climb Kings Peak, and the trail certainly has its attractions, not the least of which is avoiding the Henrys Fork crowds. In the middle section, the trail runs next to a six-mile-long deep, spectacular gorge cut by Yellowstone Creek. It's not something you'd expect, as even topographic 7.5" maps don't give any clues to its existence. Probably 90 percent of this trail is within thick, beautiful forest. During September, the fall colors are another attraction, with shimmering golden or orange-red aspen leaves making a crisp accent to the deep-green evergreen forest.

Just a few steps from the Swift Creek Trailhead you'll have to cross the river. Here, Swift Creek divides into multiple streams that have spread over a wide area. People have thrown a hodgepodge of logs across the streamlets, but you'll probably end up having to wade.

On the other side of the river crossing, at the trail junction with Swift Creek, go straight ahead (north) on the Yellowstone Trail. The first section of the trail goes generally west, and is characterized by a lot of short ascents and descents and aimless wanderings to and from the river. Because of the trail's relatively low starting point, you'll be in an interesting mixed forest of lodgepoles, aspens, ponderosas, and even sagebrush. Near the river, you'll see alders and birch.

Note that maps usually show the trail crossing the river twice, around M13.1, about three and one-half miles from the trailhead, but the current trail actually stays on the east side of the canyon.

In the six-mile-long gorge section (starting at M13.2), I recommend wandering over to the edge every now and again for a look. It's amazing. The thirty- to sixty-foot walls are splashed with colorful lichen and striped with dark water streaks. You'll notice many evergreens growing in the bottom of the gorge that are so tall that the tops are still fifty feet overhead. Other trees hang precariously off ledges. The first part of the gorge has the best views.

The gorge generally doesn't allow access to the river except where the Garfield Basin Trail crosses (M13.3), about two-thirds of the way through the gorge, where it breaks up briefly. But if you need to camp along the way, there are quite a few side streams to get water from, and even a few very nice sites overlooking the gorge.

The junction with the Garfield Basin Trail is very prominent with large signs. The Yellowstone Creek Trail goes straight ahead. The Garfield Basin Trail turns left, crosses the river, and then climbs up to Swasey Lakes. Immediately down the Garfield Basin Trail, just before reaching the river, there's a large, well-used camping area with a dozen or so possible tent sites (heaven forbid you'd ever be surrounded by a dozen other tents).

Continuing up the Yellowstone Trail from this junction, the gorge starts up again, as scenic as ever. Another two miles along brings you to the prominent junction with the trail to Bluebell Pass and Timothy Lakes (M13.4). By this time the gorge has all but disappeared.

Several minutes from the trail junction you'll reach Milk Creek. Where the trail crosses, the stream is narrow and thus very swift, but if you walk upstream into the willow clusters, you'll find an easier crossing where the water has spread out more.

Barely five minutes after Milk Creek, you'll have to cross Yellowstone Creek. In the fall you may be able to cross on boulders (as you can Milk Creek), but in early season, particularly early July, this "creek" gets very large. It can be deep and dangerously swift. If it looks too hazardous to cross, you can easily walk cross-country alongside the river all the way to the upper basin and intersect the Highline Trail there. There are no more major crossings on the Yellowstone Creek Trail (it does cross several tributaries to the Yellowstone in the upper basin, but they aren't a problem).

About two and one-half miles beyond the Yellowstone Creek crossing, the trail starts climbing more steeply, going above the river and a small gorge. You'll come out above the gorge's tall, rocky walls, and will have a fascinating view of the river thundering down through it (M13.5). The river has chopped through reddish rock layers, creating a very narrow canyon that is strangely reminiscent of some southern Utah canyons. Near this area (or very soon) you'll finally have views of Kings Peak, previously hidden behind other ridges.

Here at the gorge viewpoint, you can take the trail or a shortcut cross-country route that goes straight ahead, following the river course.

CROSS-COUNTRY SHORTCUT: 1.3 MILES

This shortcut saves you only a half mile, but you might try it if you're short on time or simply looking for an interesting cross-country route. Walking straight ahead from the gorge viewpoint (M13.5), you should find small cairns and even a small trail for a ways. This route is very straightforward, with easy walking and no major creeks to ford. You can stay on the left side of Yellowstone Creek all the way until intersecting the Highline Trail (M13.7 and M8.19). Early-season bogs may make this route less than desirable, however.

From the gorge viewpoint (M13.5), the trail turns quickly left (west), angling uphill. The trail might be hard to spot initially—you can locate it by looking for large cairns—but it quickly turns into a more prominent trail. Fifteen minutes from Yellowstone Creek, you'll have exited the forest and arrived in the upper-basin meadows, where the trail disappears completely. Following cairns and a faint trail for another fifteen minutes or so, you'll reach the junction with the Highline Trail (M13.6, M8.18, and M12.12).

The Highline Trail junction is out in the middle of the wide-open basin, with a few stunted tree clusters and willow shrubs, and most likely a small, flimsy sign. The trail to Smiths Fork Pass continues straight ahead (north). Going right (east) on the Highline Trail takes you to Anderson Pass.

TO ANDERSON PASS (HIGHLINE TRAIL): 3.5 MILES, +1690/−120 FEET

About five minutes of hiking east on a nearly straight line toward Anderson Pass, the trail descends down off the plateau. You'll cross three tributary streams to Yellowstone Creek. After the second stream you'll start passing through clusters of sizable trees. There are many scattered used campsites around here (M13.7, M8.19, and M12.13). You'll also find some good areas for dispersed camping, more so than you'd think being so high in a rocky, sloped basin. Many people use this area as a base camp for Kings Peak.

Route Segment	Miles	Gain/Loss	Time Est.
Upper-basin camping area (M12.13) to Anderson Pass	2.8	+1,690'	1.5 hr

Hiking on toward Anderson Pass, you'll cross the last tributary stream at the base of the plateau beneath Kings Peak. At the top of the plateau, you are above timberline and will have a sweeping, unobstructed view of Kings Peak and South Kings Peak towering above you. The trail fades in places, but it's pretty obvious where the trail is headed (you should be able to see the trail cutting diagonally upward to Anderson Pass, as well as cairns).

To Smiths Fork Pass (M8.9) from the Highline Trail Junction (M8.18): 2.0 miles, +680 feet

Walking up-trail from the Highline Trail junction (M10.7, M8.18, and M13.6), you'll parallel a stream for a ways, and later pass by a couple of small ponds. This high, wide-open, exposed terrain allows for some great views to the south into the Yellowstone drainage. The trail climbs gently inclined slopes the entire way (it's quite a bit faster and easier than the other side of Smiths Fork Pass). You'll travel beneath the pass for nearly one-third of a mile before finally beginning a very long switchback to the top.

Gilbert Peak, from Dollar Lake

One-way Route Summary

Reference	Miles	Gain/Loss	Time Est.	Class
Map 11, P1	2.8	+2,655	2-2.5 hrs	2

Starting from Dollar Lake, this route goes up Gilbert Peak's curved western ridge, then ascends low-angled slopes to the summit. You can also make a loop and climb Gunsight Peak. Hikers who normally avoid Uinta peaks because of boulders can do both of these summits, and still have the satisfaction of having climbed Utah's third and eighth highest (Gilbert and Gunsight, respectively).

From the Henrys Fork Trail, contour above Dollar Lake through the trees (there's no need to actually start from the lakeshore). On the south side of the lake you can find some game trails through the brush. The north side is a bit easier. Start climbing up through the trees, on steep slopes at times, into Dollar Cirque (AN). If you start up Gilbert's ridge too soon—that is, more on the west side, which is easy to do—you may end up on extremely steep slopes. It's best to climb up into the cirque until reaching the cirque flats, so you can start up the ridge on the lesser-angled east side.

You'll gain altitude quickly, but the ridge top itself has plenty of grassy vegetation and no boulder fields, so it's generally easy climbing (CL 2). The terrain rolls off hundreds of feet on either side, making the perspective on Dollar Lake especially picturesque.

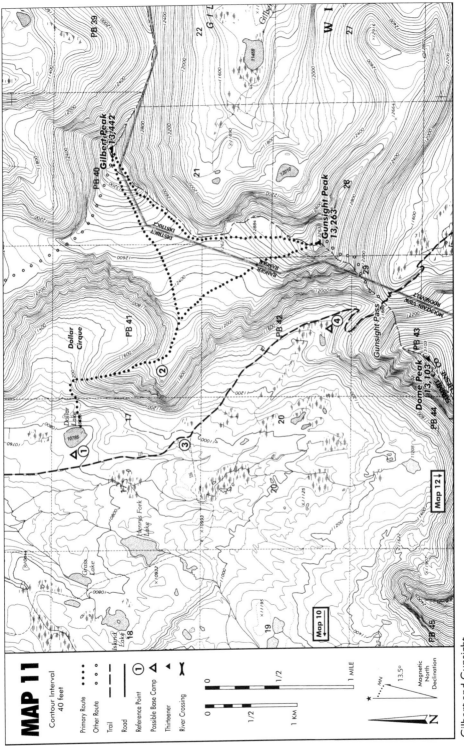

MAP 11

Contour Interval
40 feet

Primary Route ••••
Other Route ◦◦◦◦
Trail ▬ ▬ ▬
Road ▬▬▬
Reference Point ①
Possible Base Camp △
Thirteener ▲
River Crossing ⋊

0   1/2   1 KM
0   1/2   1 MILE

N

13.5°
Magnetic
North
Declination
MN

Map 10
Map 12

Gilbert Peak
13,442

Gunsight Peak
13,263

Dome Peak
13,103'

Gunsight Pass

Dollar
Cirque

Dollar
Lake

Henrys Fork
Lake

Grass
Lake

Island
Lake

RANGER DISTRICT
MOUNTAIN VIEW RANGER DISTRICT
SUMMIT COUNTY

PB 39
PB 40
PB 41
PB 42
PB 43
PB 44
PB 45

W I
G I L

22
21
28
27
29
20
19
18
17

①②③④

Gilbert and Gunsight

Gilbert Peak, view from Island Lake, Henrys Fork basin

The ridge soon connects with a gigantic plateau (M11.2) thirteen hundred feet above Dollar Lake (half the vertical elevation gain to the summit). At twelve thousand feet, this plateau is one of the highest in the Uintas. The plateau has a lot of patchy grass sections, making for easygoing hiking (CL 1).

As you climb toward the summit, you'll go over a series of large, rolling terraces, and the boulders will gradually increase in number. At some point, the slope will suddenly get steeper and turn into a boulder field, in what looks like the final summit slope. This section is about a Class 2 climb on typical boulders and turns out to be a false summit. From here you can see the real summit curving off into the distance about one-third of a mile away, over gently inclined ground with rocks and small boulders.

You should find a summit register within a rock-wall shelter. From here you can see all the 13ers, including a distant but striking view of Tokewanna Peak on the skyline—it's the large, rounded triangular shape on the northern edge of the Uintas.

Gunsight Peak, view from Island Lake, Henrys Fork basin

Gunsight Peak, from Gilbert Peak

One-way Route Summary

Reference	Miles	Gain/Loss	Time Est.	Class
Map 11	1.8	-815'/+640'	1-1.5 hr	1+

Gilbert and Gunsight are naturally climbed together. The route goes southwest from Gilbert over relatively gentle topography with a gradual, moderate elevation change.

Leaving Gilbert's summit, walk southwest down low-angled boulder slopes. You'll be near the top edge of the steep, rugged eastern face. About five to ten minutes after leaving Gilbert's summit, you'll encounter a rough but brief Class 2+ section. You can avoid this if you really want to take it easy (CL 1+) by staying away from the edge of the ridge to the west.

You'll quickly reach the wide, gentle saddle between Gilbert and Gunsight. There are several snowfields that hang around through late summer along the left (east) side of the ridge near the saddle.

Climbing up the slopes to Gunsight is similar to Gilbert Peak, with gradually increasing boulders and steepness, but the route remains easy, a Class 1+ all the way to the summit. It is very straightforward, with no surprises. Just take a direct line to the high point. The elongated summit of Gunsight has fantastic views down to the rugged cliffs and buttresses above Gunsight Pass.

Gunsight Peak Descent to Dollar Lake

One-way Route Summary

Reference	Miles	Gain/Loss	Time Est.	Class
Map 11	2.7	-2,480'	1.5 hrs	2

To descend Gunsight, you can basically head straight toward the top of the Dollar Lake ridge (M11.2) to the north, at the edge of the plateau. The descent down to the grassy flats of the plateau is a little steeper (CL 2) than the ascent route, but still easy. There should be a year-round small spring and stream at about the center of the plateau, and in late August or early September you may also see white puffy balls of cotton grass (rarely seen in the Uintas, in my experience). The feathery "cotton" strands are actually minute petals of flowers. After the flats, simply connect to the Dollar Lake ridge and retrace your original route—the descent is fast and enjoyable.

Dome Peak, from Gunsight Pass

One-way Route Summary

Reference	Miles	Gain/Loss	Time Est.	Class
Map 12	0.8	+1,215'	1 hr	2+

This climb starts from the trail at Gunsight Pass and curves up the eastern face of Dome Peak. The first part of the route follows the Gunsight Cutoff, a route that goes west from the top of Gunsight Pass and climbs to the top of the plateau beneath Dome Peak and Kings Peak. Read the end of the "Henrys Fork Trail" description for the details. Because the Gunsight Cutoff is used as a shortcut to Anderson Pass–area summits (including Kings Peak), Dome can be conveniently climbed en route (or on the way back).

Dome Peak, telephoto view from Second Gemini

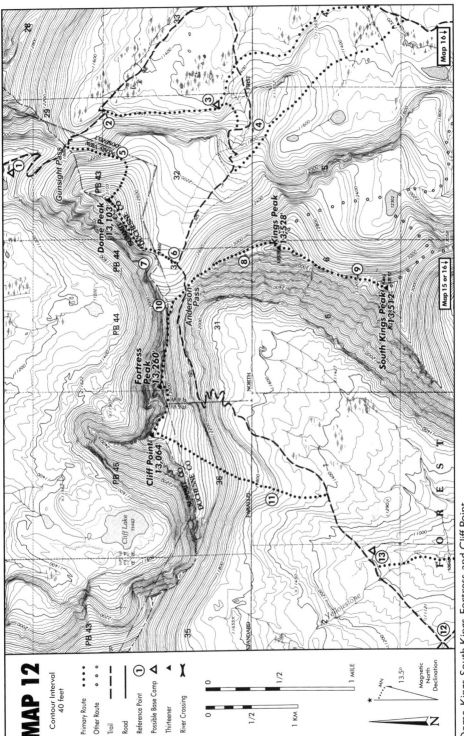

MAP 12

Contour Interval
40 feet

Primary Route
Other Route
Trail
Road
Reference Point ①
Possible Base Camp △
Thirteener ▲
River Crossing ⋈

0   1/2   1 KM
0   1/2   1 MILE

N
13.5°
MN

Magnetic
North
Declination

Dome, Kings, South Kings, Fortress, and Cliff Point

At the top of Gunsight Cutoff (M12.5), if you head straight for the summit, you'll encounter some surprisingly steep and rough slopes, getting close to Class 3+. For a much easier route (CL 2, maybe 2+), make a curved path to the left (west) as you climb. You'll then be able to walk up the rounded bulge or ridge leading up to the summit. The boulders are generally stable with a moderate slope angle. The summit of Dome Peak is relatively spacious, and the northern side drops off onto loose and rugged slopes. From the summit, the perspective of Fortress Peak with its sheer one thousand–foot north face is incredible.

Dome Peak, from Anderson Pass

One-way Route Summary

Reference	Miles	Gain/Loss	Time Est.	Class
Map 12	0.8	-250'/+665'	45 min	1+ or 2

Coming from Anderson Pass, the west ridge of Dome Peak is the obvious choice. It's a simple route, significantly easier than the route from Gunsight Pass.

Hike east down the Highline Trail to the flats (plateau) (M12.6) just below Anderson Pass. Leave the trail and head toward the base of Dome's west ridge. You can leave the trail anywhere in the flats and take almost any route up to the west ridge without difficulty. The slopes are all about Class 1+ to 2 on soil or small rocks. Near the beginning of the ridge, you'll have a near bird's-eye view of a steep chute (M12.7) that some people attempt as a shortcut from the Henrys Fork basin (it's dangerous and not recommended). The route along the ridge top to the summit is a fast Class 1 to 1+ with a short, slightly rougher section near the summit. Along the way, you'll have fantastic views of Fortress Peak and Dome's rugged northwest face.

Kings Peak, from Anderson Pass

One-way Route Summary

Reference	Miles	Gain/Loss	Time Est.	Class
Map 12	0.7	+840'	45-60 min	2+

Utah's tallest peak is a short, moderate climb from Anderson Pass. This route leaves the trail and climbs south on or near the ridge top to the summit. You can then continue along the ridge to South Kings Peak.

There's no established trail to the summit of Kings Peak, but you'll come across paths that have been worn into the mountain by the many people who

Kings Peak (center skyline) looms above hikers on the Henrys Fork Trail

have been there before. In fact, you'll probably see a faint trail right away, heading up the ridge from Anderson Pass. The trail soon dissipates into multiple paths you can follow as you climb through the maze of boulders. The main paths stay off the ridge to the left (east), ascending and traversing the slopes. But you could also climb the ridge top, being careful of the west-face cliff exposure. On the way down, the bottom half of the ridge top is a little easier and faster to boulder-hop than the slopes. Any way you go, the first half of the climb is generally straightforward Class 2 to 2+ climbing.

At about the midpoint, a twenty-five-foot cliff promontory comes into view on the ridge crest (M12.8). The right (west) side of this promontory has weathered into a pinnacle, and the level ridge abreast of it offers a chance for a break among some colorful yellow angular rocks. Early on, this cliff promontory isn't obvious, but during the climb it creates a false summit. The actual summit is just another ten to fifteen minutes away.

After the promontory, the ridge crest gets more rugged (CL 3), with some higher fifty-plus-foot cliffs off the west side. The easier way is to stay well off the ridge and traverse southerly beneath the ridge crest on Class 2+ boulders (judging by well-worn climbing paths, most other hikers agree). Once you're beneath the summit, make a straight shot up to the top.

There are a couple of high points on the summit block of Kings Peak. The

Kings Peak, view from Upper Yellowstone basin

highest of the points isn't exactly spacious, but still has room enough to sit and enjoy the view. It's an impressive-looking summit with fifty- to seventy-five-foot cliffs that drop directly off the west side. And there are of course the sweeping views that you'd expect standing at the top of Utah. On clear days, you can see seventy miles to the Wasatch Range.

South Kings Peak, from Kings Peak

One-way Route Summary

Reference	Miles	Gain/Loss	Time Est.	Class
Map 12	0.8	-450'/+435'	45 min	2

If you can pull yourself away from Utah's highest point, you're in a great position to climb the second highest, South Kings Peak. The ridge to South Kings has several minor ups and downs, or "bumps," the last of which (M12.9) makes a definite false summit.

From Kings Peak, go south down the ridge top. The first section is easy (CL 1+), with lots of flat rocks you can hop across. You'll go over a little swell, hardly noticeable, that turns into a brief false summit coming back to Kings.

After some Class 2 down-climbing, you'll reach the first low point in the ridge, before the first bump. Traverse around the left (east) side of the bump on

South Kings Peak (right skyline), view from Kings Peak

flat, large rocks (CL 2). Go around the next bump the same way, traversing on even easier terrain.

Climbing up average Class 2 boulders, you'll reach the false summit (M12.9) in probably five to ten minutes, and about five minutes later the actual summit of South Kings Peak. It's a fairly large, gently rounded summit. There should be a summit register on top. A Forest Service marker dated 1981 interestingly labels the peak simply King. You have a great view of Kings Peak from here; you'll be able to see the tiny figures of other climbers on the summit if they are standing upright against the sky. To the south, the Geminis and other Group 4 summits are easily visible along the Kings-Emmons ridge.

Fortress Peak, from Anderson Pass

One-way Route Summary

Reference	Miles	Gain/Loss	Time Est.	Class
Map 12	0.7	+570′	30-45 min	3+

This route is a classic, featuring a spectacular ridge-top scramble and an airy summit perch. Fortress Peak is the fastest summit to reach from Anderson Pass. From the summit, you can continue west along the ridge to Cliff Point, another 13er. If you're coming from the Yellowstone drainage, you could then

Fortress Peak and Cliff Point, view from Dome Peak

turn the entire hike into a loop by descending south from Cliff Point to the Highline Trail.

The first section of the route is a fun Class 2+ boulder-hop to Anderson Knob (M12.10). At the knob, make an ascending traverse around it, on looser angular rocks, to the beginning of Fortress's east ridge.

The cliffs beneath the ridge are both unnerving and breathtaking. Several parts of the ridge top are only three to five feet wide. The left (south) side has piles of huge boulders, and the right (north) side is a vertical plunge for fifty feet before dropping another six hundred feet at extreme angles. In other places the ridge is overhung. There are some Class 3+ moves, depending on where you choose to go, but most of it is closer to Class 2+. Proximity to cliffs makes this route potentially dangerous. On the ridge crest, you may have to hop across deep crevices or boulders near the cliff edge. Be careful and use good judgment. You can always scramble off the ridge onto less-exposed terrain.

The narrowest parts of the ridge don't last very long. The ridge top turns spiky and rough, making it better to get off the ridge and traverse to the left (CL 2). Getting back onto the ridge, you'll hike through a brief easy section, ending at the base of the summit mound. The best way up the summit mound is a short scramble up and around the left (south) side, on loose soil and rock (CL 2+). Going directly up the ridgeline is harder (CL 3), on unstable boulders.

In keeping with the extremes of the approach ridge, the summit of Fortress Peak covers a tiny area, only about ten to fifteen feet around. The north- and northwest-face cliffs drop off about eight hundred feet from the summit, and include a striking yellowish fin of rock. To the west, a wave of massive cliff faces begins at the summit and goes to Cliff Point, Mount Powell, and Wilson Peak. Uinta summits rarely get better than this.

Fortress Peak, view from Cliff Point

Cliff Point, from Fortress Peak

One-way Route Summary

Reference	Miles	Gain/Loss	Time Est.	Class
Map 12	0.4	-230'/+35'	20 min	3 (4)

Continuing west from Fortress Peak, Cliff Point is literally just minutes away, really more like a descent than a climb. The top of the ridge is a jagged knife-edge, but there's a handy way around it.

From Fortress Peak, start climbing down directly from the summit, angling to the right toward the base of the west-ridge cliffs. You'll encounter a short (maybe ten-foot) Class 4 section; otherwise, it's about Class 3. When you reach the bottom of the cliffs, traverse at the base (CL 2+). The traverse is brief. You'll suddenly pop out onto an easy, very gentle Class 1 ridge with soil and small rocks. Simply follow this flat and rounded ridge to the high point of Cliff Point.

Cliff Point (center) and Mount Powell (center skyline), view from Fortress Peak

Standing on Cliff Point, you'll have more great views to the west of layer upon layer of incredible ridges and summits. The peak has an exceptionally impressive north face. There's a vertical 400-foot cliff face on the northern edge, which is actually more easily seen from Fortress Peak. Looking back toward Fortress Peak, you'll notice an interesting geological feature: a sudden change in bedrock color, from Fortress's light yellow to Cliff Point's reddish bands.

Cliff Point Descent to Upper Yellowstone

To	Miles	Gain/Loss	Time Est.	Class
Upper Yellowstone camping area (M12.13)	1.8	-2,065'	1 hr	2+

To Highline Trail: 1.3 miles, -1,665', 45 min

This route is the shorter, easier way to return to the Yellowstone drainage. The alternative is of course to retrace your route back to Anderson Pass and hike down the Highline Trail.

The route starts down Cliff Point's southwest slopes, which gradually turn into a broad ridge. The terrain is so broad at first that it's a little difficult to tell where you are positioned, so a good point of reference is to head straight toward the distant treeline at the edge of the western Kings plateau. Using this line, you'll avoid a cliff band at about the halfway point. Most of the route is on easy to moderate, partly vegetated Class 1 or 1+ slopes.

Near the bottom, you'll reach a grassy shelf above a long, somewhat broken, old cliff band (M12.11) that extends along the base of the mountain. There are many ways to get down, about Class 2 or 2+, keeping in mind that the cliff gets higher as you go left (east). Some enormous blocklike boulders have accumulated in piles at the bottom of the cliff band and require some fun scrambling.

This route would also be a good way to *ascend* Cliff Point and Fortress Peak from upper Yellowstone. Going up, you'll have an easier time picking out a route through the cliffs because you have the full view of it from the trail.

GROUP 4: South Slope Summits

- Mount Emmons: 13,440 feet (#4)
- First Gemini (AN): 13,387 feet (#5)
- Second Gemini (AN): 13,306 feet (#6)
- Pyramid Peak (AN): 13,287 feet (#7)
- Ramp Peak (AN): 13,247 feet (#10)
- Glacier Peak (AN): 13,170 feet (#12)
- Pinnacle Peak (AN): 13,068 feet (#17)

All the peaks in this Group are situated on the same long, continuous ridge in the heart of the Uinta Mountains. Positioned one after the other, these seven summits start at Glacier Peak (just south of Emmons) and end at Second Gemini. This massive ridgeline actually originates at Flat Top Mountain near the southern wilderness boundary and extends northward for thirteen miles to South Kings Peak and Kings Peak (described in Group 3). The highest ridge section is often referred to as the Kings-Emmons ridge.

The two best ways to access Group 4 summits are the Swift Creek Trail (see Map 13) and the Atwood Basin Trail (see Map 14). Both trails are rigorous hikes, starting more than one thousand feet lower than the north-slope trailheads. The Atwood Trail is longer than the Swift Creek Trail (by six miles) with more elevation gain (eighteen hundred more feet). It's doable in a long, tiring one-day backpack, but you could split it into an easier two days by camping at the Chain Lakes area.

The Swift Creek basin is steep and compact, and seems to be more rugged and rocky than other basins. It's a magnificent, scenic area, dominated and sandwiched on the east and north by the towering Kings-Emmons ridge. As a sort of testament to this rugged country, the upper basin supports a healthy population of mountain goats.

The Atwood Basin Trail approach offers a taste of everything: riverside hiking, deep forest, exceptionally long switchbacks, a big rocky pass, many scenic lakes, and great alpine basin camping. The peaks from Atwood are visually more impressive than from Swift Creek, with a sweeping side view of the entire

View from Pyramid Peak: Ramp Peak, Second Gemini, South Kings Peak, First Gemini, Kings Peak

Kings-Emmons ridge. Lake Atwood is an absolutely enormous lake, a good fit for the Uinta River drainage, which could be the largest in the Uintas.

The climbs here are divided into two main groups. The first is Pinnacle Peak, Mount Emmons, and Glacier Peak—what I call the Emmons Loop. The second group is Ramp Peak, First Gemini, Second Gemini, and Pyramid Peak.

For many reasons (including positioning and easy ridge walks versus rough slopes), the Emmons Loop summits are naturally climbed together, from either Atwood or Swift Creek. The easiest way to climb Mount Emmons itself is from Atwood Basin. In fact, the entire loop from Lake Atwood is an enjoyable day, somewhat easier than from Swift Creek (also, the route from Swift Creek doesn't make a full loop unless you take a harder alternative descent).

A grouping strategy is also very sensible for the other four summits: Ramp Peak, First Gemini, Second Gemini, and Pyramid Peak. Ramp Peak and the Geminis are connected by easy, low-angled ridges, and there is really no better route option for the Geminis than going over Ramp Peak first. It is most convenient to add Pyramid to the day's itinerary if you can—making it a long day—but it is perfectly prudent to do Pyramid Peak separately. Let weather, time, and energy decide that one for you. Climbing all four peaks from Swift Creek—Pyramid first, followed by Ramp and the Geminis—is a bit easier and more natural than from Atwood, where you'd have to climb over the summit of Ramp an extra time.

Mount Emmons and Pinnacle Peak, view from near Lake Atwood

The Bluebell Pass Trail (see Map 13) is described in this section. It's included here because it makes a handy connecting trail from Swift Creek to the Yellowstone Creek Trail, which you can use to access other 13ers in Group 2 (Mount Powell and Wilson Peak) or Group 3 (Kings Peak and others) on an extended trip. Or you could simply use it to make an interesting loop trip, beginning and ending at the Swift Creek Trailhead. Note that the Yellowstone Creek Trail is described in Group 3 as an access to Kings Peak and surrounding summits.

Estimated Time for an All-Inclusive Trip: four to six days (not including rest days, bad weather days, or driving time)

Trailhead Information

Driving directions, parking and campground information are detailed in the "Driving to the Trailheads" section. To drive to the Swift Creek Trailhead, see page 48. To get to the Uinta Trailhead (Atwood Basin Trail), see page 49.

Trail and Round-Trip Route Summaries

Swift Creek Trail (Map 13)

TRAILHEAD: Swift Creek, Elev. 8,115'
TIME ESTIMATE: 6.5 hrs to East Timothy Lake

Destination (one-way)	Miles	Elevation	Elev. Gain
East Timothy Lake (M13.13)	9.0	11,020'	+2,905'

Atwood Basin Trail (Map 14)

TRAILHEAD: Uinta, Elev. 7,720'
TIME ESTIMATE: 11 hrs to Lake Atwood

Destination (one-way)	Miles	Elevation	Elev. Gain
Middle Chain Lake (M14.3)	9.5	10,620'	+2,900'
Roberts Pass (M14.4)	11.0	11,140'	+3,420'
Lake Atwood (M14.7)	15.0	11,020'	+3,920'/–620'
Trail Rider Pass (M14.8)	18.0	11,790'	+4,690'/–620'

Round-Trip Routes

Peaks: Starting Points	Elev. Gain	Miles	Time Est.	Grade
Ramp, Geminis (Map 15 or 16)				
East Timothy Lake (M15.1)	+2,810'	9.0	5.5 hrs	III
Lake Atwood (M16.1)	+3,335'	11.2	6.5 hrs	III
TRAILHEAD (Swift Creek—M13)	+5,715'	27.0	—	—
TRAILHEAD (Uinta—M14)	+7,875'	41.2	—	—
Ramp, Geminis, Pyramid (Map 15 or 16)				
East Timothy Lake (M15.1)	+3,360'	10.4	7 hrs	IV
Lake Atwood (M16.1)	+3,880'	10.9	8 hrs	IV
TRAILHEAD (Swift Creek—M13)	+6,265'	28.4	—	—
TRAILHEAD (Uinta—M14)	+8,420'	40.9	—	—
Pyramid Peak (Map 15 or 16)				
East Timothy Lake (M15.1)	+2,265'	7.2	5 hrs	II
Lake Atwood (M16.1)	+2,265'	5.4	4.5 hrs	II
TRAILHEAD (Swift Creek—M13)	+5,170'	25.2	—	—
TRAILHEAD (Uinta—M14)	+6,805'	35.4	—	—
Emmons, Glacier, Pinnacle (Map 17 or 18)				
East Timothy Lake (M18.1)	+3,170'	8.0	6 hrs	III
Lake Atwood (M17.1)	+3,170'	7.8	6 hrs	III
TRAILHEAD (Swift Creek—M13)	+6,075'	26.0	—	—
TRAILHEAD (Uinta—M14)	+7,710'	37.8	—	—
Mount Emmons (Map 17 or 18)				
East Timothy Lake (M18.1)	+2,420'	6.2	4.5 hrs	II
Lake Atwood (M17.1)	+2,420'	6.0	4 hrs	II
TRAILHEAD (Swift Creek—M13)	+5,325'	24.2	—	—
TRAILHEAD (Uinta—M14)	+6,960'	36.0	—	—

Mount Emmons (left) and Glacier Peak (right), view from upper Swift Creek basin

Swift Creek Trail

Map point	M13.8	M13.9	M13.10	M13.11	M13.12	M13.13	M13.14
Miles from trailhead	3.5	4.5	5.8	6.4	8.0	9.0	10.0

Just a few steps from the Swift Creek Trailhead, you'll have to cross the river. Here, Swift Creek divides into multiple streams that have spread over a wide area. People have thrown a hodgepodge of logs across the streamlets, but you'll probably end up having to wade.

Directly on the other side of the crossing, the trail divides. A sign points straight ahead to Yellowstone (this trail is described in Group 3). Turn right, following another sign that points right (east) to Swift Creek.

The first half of the Swift Creek Trail is quite rocky, so good campsites with water access are scarce. There are a *few* sites around the next two creek crossings (M13.8 and M13.9), but abundant campsites aren't available until you're a mile beyond Deer Lake.

The Swift Creek Trail (#056 on Forest Service maps) quickly starts ascending, going up about seven dry, rocky switchbacks, which make for a sweaty summer climb. You'll first ascend through ponderosa and scattered juniper (a rare thing for High Uinta trails), but the forest quickly gives way to the standard lodgepole. The switchbacks end on a very interesting ridge—the trail

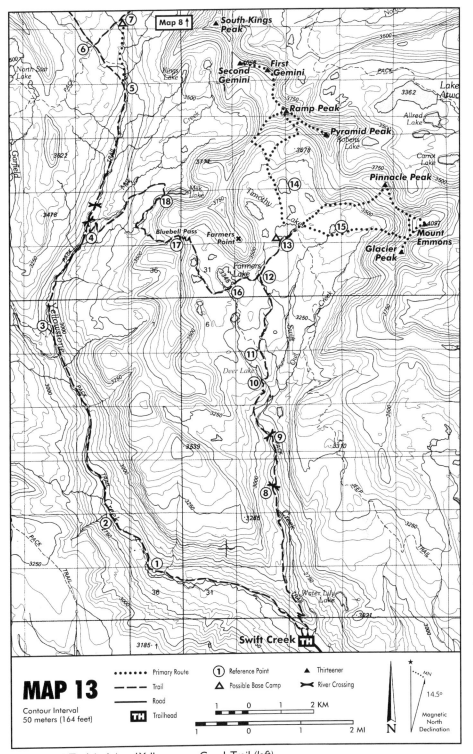

Swift Creek Trail *(right)* and Yellowstone Creek Trail *(left)*

follows the crest, which is surprisingly narrow at times and blanketed with a dizzying amount of slender lodgepoles. The views into the Yellowstone Creek drainage are tremendous, showcasing the massive size of Uinta forestland.

After the ridge, you'll continue climbing, eventually going down a short, steep, rocky descent to Swift Creek. In about ten minutes you'll pass by an old, large beaver dam, apparently abandoned, and a few minutes later you'll reach the second major stream crossing (M13.8). This crossing can be an intimidating, raging torrent in early season. The best wading route is immediately upstream from where the trail crosses, where the river has divided into two smaller parts. However, you might be able to avoid wading altogether by walking down-trail to the aforementioned beaver dam. Directly on the other side (east) of the dam, you should find a cluster of sturdy logs spanning a narrow part of the river.

After the crossing, the trail makes its way above the river, and descends to another old beaver dam, crossing a streamlet that flows into the pond. Soon afterward, you'll reach the third river crossing (M13.9), only a mile after the previous one. During late-season trips you might be able to just hop across on boulders, but in early season you'll probably have to wade.

Shortly after the third river crossing, you'll cross a sizable side stream, coming in on your left (west), on a solid log walkway. From here you're very near Deer Lake. The trail makes about six widely spread switchbacks before topping out, and about ten minutes later you'll be at Deer Lake (M13.10).

About twenty minutes or a half mile past Deer Lake, you will come to a trail junction (M13.11) deep in the forest. A sign points left to Farmers Lake and Bluebell Pass, and another points right to Timothy Lake. Take the right-hand trail to Timothy Lakes.

Walking twenty minutes past the trail junction, you'll come to a meadow with a pond, where the trail fades almost completely. Follow the left (west) edge of this meadow. Then cut across the upper end of the meadow to the right (east) and enter the forest, where you should find the trail again. The forest ends shortly, at the entrance to another large meadow (at the time of this writing, it was distinguished by two posts to the side of the trail). Again the trail fades as it passes through the meadow, but if you stay on the left (west) edge, you'll see the trail just before entering the trees again.

Just over an hour or so from the trail junction (M13.11), you'll exit the forest and immediately thereafter reach another trail junction (M13.12), located at the edge of a large, marshy meadow at the base of rocky, rounded Farmers Point (AN). The trail straight ahead goes to Timothy Lakes. The other trail goes to Farmers Lake and Bluebell Pass. Historically, this junction hasn't been marked well, so be alert if you're looking for the Bluebell Pass Trail (refer to "Bluebell Pass Trail" description).

Taking the trail straight ahead to Timothy Lakes, you'll continue alongside the marshy meadow, and after a bit of climbing, East Timothy Lake will come into view.

East Timothy Lake (M13.13) is a good central location for all the climbs in this basin. Good campsites are on the west side of the lake. In my opinion, you'll find some of the best campsites in the basin—although less central to the summits—on the eastern side of the basin, closer to Mount Emmons. No maintained trails go into the area, so you'll have privacy, and dispersed camping would give high-use areas a break. One possibility is near Emmons Lake (AN) (M13.15; see also Map 18 for details), which is about three-quarters of a mile due east of East Timothy Lake, over easy terrain, with easy route-finding.

Upper Carrol Lake (M13.14; see also Map 15 for details) is an option closer to Pyramid, Ramp, and the Geminis. From East Timothy Lake, it will take approximately thirty to forty minutes with a pack. The ground surrounding Carrol tends to be very boggy and rocky. The south and northwest sides are your best bets for camping.

Atwood Basin Trail

Map point	M14.1	M14.2	M14.3	M14.4	M14.5	M14.6	M14.7	M14.8
Miles from trailhead	3.5	7.5	9.5	11.0	12.7	14.0	15.0	17.5

This relatively long trail goes a short distance up the Uinta River, climbs west into Krebs Basin (in the Chain Lakes area) (M14.3) and goes over Roberts Pass (M14.4) before finally reaching the Atwood Basin (M14.7). If desired, you can continue over Trail Rider Pass (M14.8) and into Painter Basin.

From the Uinta Trailhead parking area, walk up the dirt road for just over half a mile to the small day-use and fishermen's parking lot. Refer to "Driving to the Trailheads" for details on the parking and car-camping situation. There is actually a trail winding up from the Uinta Trailhead to the day-use parking lot, but it takes longer to walk than the road. The hiking trail begins on the northeast side of the parking lot. The trail passes above Smokey Spring pond and through a gate, and the hike begins.

If you're planning on camping along the first half of the trail, your best bets for convenient, reliable water and decent camping are either at the Sheep Bridge crossing (M14.1) or at Krebs Creek (M14.2). Sheep Bridge is three miles from the trailhead. Krebs Creek has better camping, but it is 7.5 miles from the trailhead and gains 2,300 feet in elevation.

The easygoing trail to Sheep Bridge goes through pleasant, pretty country, alternating mixed forest (aspen, spruce, and Douglas fir), aspen stands, and riparian vegetation. You'll also see plenty of beaver activity. The environment is in good condition, thanks to the apparent lack of cattle.

There's a trail junction just before Sheep Bridge. The Highline Trail is fifteen miles straight ahead. Go left on the trail to Atwood Basin and cross the Uinta River on the bridge. It's a very sturdy steel-framed bridge, well above the river, one of the few bridges you can really count on being there for a good long while.

Hiking straight ahead on the other side of the bridge, you'll immediately start the long climb out of the canyon. There are about a dozen big switchbacks, one of them a third of a mile long, that take you more than eight hundred feet above the Uinta River. The good thing is that the switchbacks are very efficient (not too steep, not too flat), and the trail isn't very rocky, so it'll go relatively fast. Also, the thick forest provides relief from the sun.

After the switchbacks, you'll be hiking on a forested bench. You'll cross a couple of small streamlets (probably only in early summer) and climb steadily on a rocky trail. At times, you can see an old, faint bulldozer path from the lake dam-building era. Eventually, you will reach the Krebs Creek crossing on two sturdy logs (a sign says Krebs Basin) (M14.2).

The trail continues with significant climbing, shortly passing by Lily Lake (barely visible through the trees). In another mile, you'll reach the multiple streamlets of the Lower Chain Lake outlet. You can pick your way across on rocks and logs.

In a welcome break from the steady climbing, you'll pass by the right side of the picturesque first three lower Chain Lakes (M14.3) and many used campsites. Unless you're really watching, you'll miss where one lake begins and another ends.

Before long, you're climbing on switchbacks again toward Roberts Pass (M14.4; see also Map 17 for details). Fourth Chain Lake, nestled into the mountainside exactly halfway up Roberts Pass, is in rocky country, but it still has some acceptable camping areas and is quite attractive. Roberts Pass is somewhat deceptive. It can be tough, especially if you're doing this entire trail in one day. It is very rocky and eroded at times, with a lot of switchbacks (more than twenty on the north side). It climbs about 475 feet, and drops 620 feet through some impressive glacial moraines with large boulders.

At the bottom of Roberts Pass, you may find a spring (could be dry by midsummer) coming from underneath an enormous boulder and running across the trail. Almost a mile of climbing later, you'll cross the small Carrot Lake

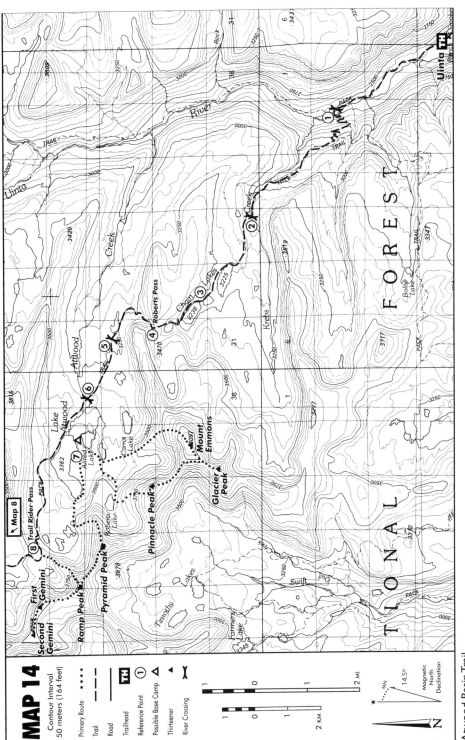

Atwood Basin Trail

View from Lake Atwood: Pyramid Peak, Ramp Peak, and First Gemini

Creek (M14.5). Afterward, the trail swings around to the northeast and eventually makes its way to a large meadow or marsh. Here, a sign points toward Lake Atwood and the Atwood Creek crossing (M14.6; see also Map 17 for details) just ahead on a double log bridge. After the meadow, you'll climb alongside the Atwood stream outlet for half a mile and reach Atwood dam.

Great camping spots are plentiful throughout the entire basin and around the lakes, but Allred and Allen Lakes and the southern shores of Atwood (M14.7; see also Maps 16 and 17) are the most central to the summit routes. Due to marshes and hilly country, the best way to get to Allred Lake (and probably Allen Lake) is to stay on the trail until Lake Atwood, then go cross-country.

Route Segment	Miles	Gain/Loss	Time Est.
Lake Atwood (M16.1) to Trail Rider Pass	3.0	+770'	1.5 hrs

The trail to the pass contours around near the shores of Lake Atwood until the northernmost point and then starts climbing. It tops out in open country, going through bouldered meadows and skirting the right side of a small lake. The trail fades, but you can follow cairns. After a handful of moderate switchbacks, you'll arrive at the top of the pass. On the way, you can examine the entire

Ramp-Pyramid route. The top of the pass holds several very scenic lakes, ringed with snow in early summer.

To Group 3 Summits, from Trail Rider Pass

The trail winds around the top of the barren, bouldered pass and then switchbacks down to the floor of Painter Basin. From there, you can go north cross-country in Painter Basin to save a significant distance (one to two miles if you're going to Gunsight or Anderson Pass). The terrain is easy and flexible. Plan your route while you still have the view from Trail Rider Pass (see overview of Maps 8 and 14 and detail of Maps 12 and 16).

If you're going to Anderson Pass, one idea is to follow the trail until it crosses the first streamlet or marsh (in about a half mile), and then head toward the low, rounded ridge in line with Dome Peak. You can follow this minor ridge until intersecting the Highline Trail on the high plateau below Anderson Pass. Going this way, Kings Peak is four and one-half miles one-way from Trail Rider Pass, and about fourteen and one-half miles round-trip from Lake Atwood.

If you're backpacking to Henrys Fork from Trail Rider Pass, continue down the trail after Trail Rider Pass, and after the second streamlet or marsh crossing (or whenever it seems appropriate), cut across the meadows toward Gunsight Pass. Eventually, you'll reach the Highline Trail.

Bluebell Pass Trail

Map point	M13.16	M13.17	M13.18	M13.4
Miles from trailhead	0.7	2.5	4.5	7.0

The Bluebell Pass Trail (#055 on Forest Service maps) actually originates at the Jackson Park Trailhead many miles to the southeast. The seven-mile-long portion I describe is sometimes called the Farmers Lake Trail. It starts at a junction with the Swift Creek Trail, passes by Farmers Lake, climbs 780 feet to Bluebell Pass (at 11,620 feet), then drops 1,660 feet to the Yellowstone Creek Trail.

The starting point (the Swift Creek Trail junction, M13.12) is located in the south end of a meadow at the base of Farmers Point. The junction hasn't been marked well in the past, and the trail is faint at first. From the junction, the trail goes southwest briefly, then cuts to the west, crossing the outlet stream of a small, marshy pond.

After the pond, the trail is easier to see. You'll ascend the tree-covered knoll extending from Farmers Peak (along the way passing through an interesting section of trail through a boulder field), before coming to Farmers Lake. About five minutes after Farmers Lake, you'll come to another junction (M13.16) next to a small creek. A branch of the Swift Creek Trail (#056 on Forest Service maps) goes left (south) downhill to Deer Lake. Continue straight ahead.

The trail begins to curve north. You'll hike for some time through the trees, and then pass through a series of meadows and by several lakes. The trail often fades in the meadows, but you should see cairns to follow.

The area just before and beneath Bluebell Pass is a beautiful place in early summer, with vibrant green alpine grass (almost like a lawn), sparkling ponds, and contrasting heaps of boulders. Soak it in, because the trail over the pass gets ugly—you'll climb up twenty-three short, steep, tiring switchbacks on a badly eroded trail with much loose gravel before reaching the top (M13.17). The trail down the other side is much the same for the first fifteen minutes or so.

About thirty minutes from the top of the pass, you'll enter forestland, and shortly thereafter a wet, marshy meadow with a pond to the left. The trail fades completely as it crosses the meadow, then turns sharply to the right (northeast), following the left edge of a long, narrow meadow with marsh grass.

You'll soon come to the edge of boulder fields coming down from the high ridges. A few small, somewhat silt-laden springs run out from under the boulders and pool up in small meadows. The trail contours at the edge of the boulders for a while, and eventually veers away and follows the left (west) edge of a meadow with a small, beautiful, meandering stream.

At the end of the meadow, there's a trail junction (M13.18) in close proximity to some heavily used campsites. The dead-end trail to Milk Lake turns right (east) and crosses two streams. The trail to Yellowstone Creek seems to disappear. To find it, cut left (west) away from the streams and walk through the campsite area. You should quickly see the trail again.

The trail immediately drops down through the trees to the edge of a huge meadow. Note that the trail turns very abruptly left (southwest) away from the meadow. Follow the tree blazes. You'll begin hiking through a beautiful, thick forest of lodgepole pines.

Eventually, you'll end up walking above a huge canyon with a roaring stream. The trail goes southwest, slightly downhill, giving the unsettling sensation that you're going down Yellowstone Creek. Rest assured that the canyon stream is Milk Creek, and if you watch carefully through the trees, later you'll see the larger Yellowstone Canyon merging with Milk Creek. (In any case, the upcoming junction with the Yellowstone Creek Trail is very prominent, with large signs. You can't miss it.)

Nearing the trail's end, you'll plunge down another very steep, badly

Ramp Peak and Pyramid Peak reflected in East Timothy Lake

eroded, loose, and rocky trail. If the trail over Bluebell Pass didn't test your knees, patience, and energy, this section surely will. Eventually, the descent ends, at the junction with the Yellowstone Creek Trail (M13.4).

Ramp Peak, from East Timothy Lake

One-way Route Summary

Reference	Miles	Gain/Loss	Time Est.	Class
Map 15, P1	3.2	+2,225'	2-2.5 hrs	2

The first part of this moderate route ascends a half-mile-wide bench or ramp that circles at the head of the Swift Creek basin (see Map 15). At the top of the bench (M15.3), the route splits: one climbs to Ramp Peak, the other to Pyramid Peak. From the summit of Ramp Peak, you can continue north along the ridge to First and Second Geminis.

You can start on either side of East Timothy Lake. The east side is slightly easier, on nearly level terrain—cross Timothy's inlet stream right away, then follow the drainage to Upper Carrol Lake and up to the bench (M15.2). If you start from the west side of Timothy, you'll immediately begin climbing forested and meadowed hills that eventually connect to the bench. You'll want to avoid dropping onto Center or West Timothy's rocky and chaparral-choked slopes.

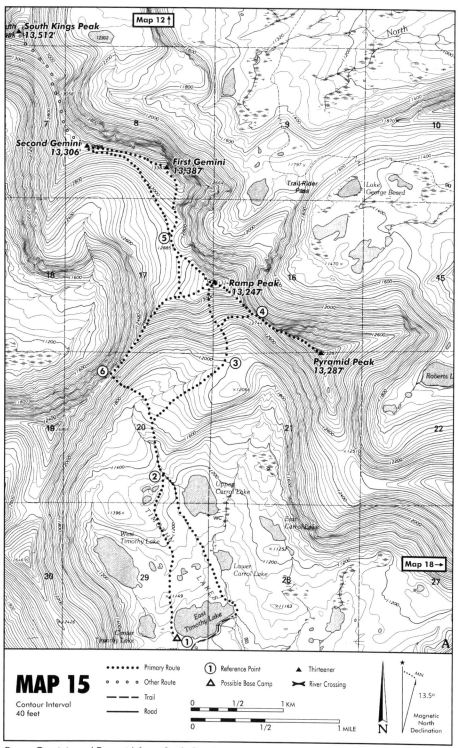

Map 12 ↑

South Kings Peak
13,512'

12302

Second Gemini
13,306'

First Gemini
13,387'

North

Trail Rider Pass

Lake George Beard

Ramp Peak
13,247'

⑤

⑥

③

④

Pyramid Peak
13,287'

Roberts L

⑳

②

Upper Carrol Lake

WC

East Carrol Lake

Map 18 →

West Timothy Lake

Lower Carrol Lake

East Timothy Lake
△ ①

Center Timothy Lake

MAP 15

Contour Interval
40 feet

•••••• Primary Route
∘∘∘∘ Other Route
– – – Trail
——— Road

① Reference Point
△ Possible Base Camp

▲ Thirteener
⨯ River Crossing

0   1/2   1 KM

0   1/2   1 MILE

N

MN
13.5°

Magnetic
North
Declination

Ramp, Geminis, and Pyramid, from Swift Creek

As you hike up the bench, you'll notice the easiest path follows the stream course, but you can obviously take a more direct line. The top of the bench is a large, high-altitude (12,000-foot) meadow. Be on the lookout for a herd of mountain goats that likes to hang out in this area.

The boulders coming down from Ramp Peak have spread into a reddish fan, ending at the meadow's edge. You can start up at any point, but you'll probably notice there's a natural route—a more moderate part of the slope that extends in a pathlike manner directly toward the summit. This slope is a solid Class 2 route, and gains about 1,200 feet. It gets somewhat steeper near the top, but overall this is a fast route with no really rough areas. You'll probably end up slightly west of the summit. The actual high point is just a mound on the ridge top. Another viable way to the summit is to veer to the right as you climb and intersect Ramp's eastern ridge (moderate, CL 2+) that connects to Pyramid.

Ramp Peak, from Trail Rider Pass (Atwood Basin)

One-way Route Summary

Reference	Miles	Gain/Loss	Time Est.	Class
Map 16	1.0	+1,455	1 hr 15 min	2+ or 3

Starting conveniently from the trail on Trail Rider Pass, this is a short, interesting, and straightforward route. It's clearly the best way to climb Ramp Peak from the Atwood Basin side. It gains a lot of elevation quickly and involves a bit of moderate scrambling.

The summit of Ramp Peak is the main takeoff point to First and Second Geminis and Pyramid Peak. From Pyramid, you can descend back to Atwood via the west ridge.

Starting from the pass, start climbing west up the ridge leading to Ramp Peak. The first half (distance-wise) of the route is easy (CL 1 or 1+). You'll hike over several alternating sections of flat-lying boulders and patchy grass with flowers. There's an almost grassy path you can follow near the edge of the ridge.

The ridge will suddenly get steeper (M16.2), and at the same time you'll start climbing boulders (CL 2 to 2+). The boulders are mostly quite stable—which is a good thing because about halfway up, the ridge angle gets even steeper, with a few Class 3 scrambling sections. The rough boulders slow your progress, but before long you'll be standing on the summit.

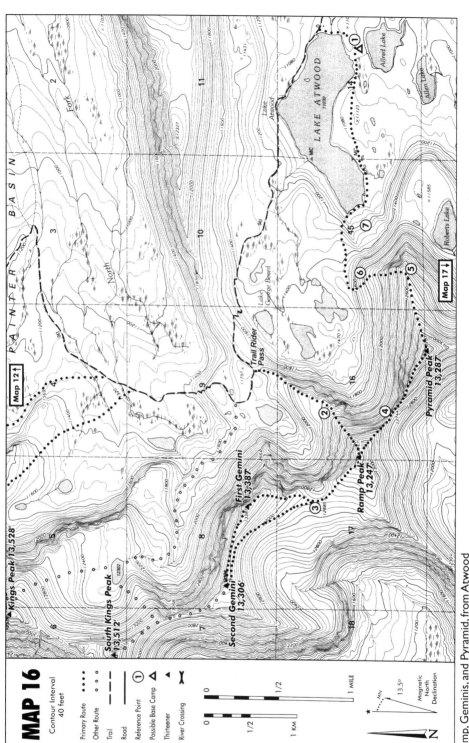

MAP 16

Contour Interval
40 feet

Primary Route ••••
Other Route ○ ○ ○
Trail — — —
Road ━━━
① Reference Point
△ Possible Base Camp
▲ Thirteener
✕ River Crossing

0 ··· 1/2 ··· 1 KM
0 ··· 1/2 ··· 1 MILE

13.5°
Magnetic
North
Declination

P A I N T E R   B A S I N

North Fork

▲ Kings Peak 13,528'

▲ South Kings Peak 13,512'

Second Gemini 13,306

First Gemini 13,387

Ramp Peak 13,247

Trail Rider Pass

Lake George Beard

Pyramid Peak 13,287

Roberts Lake

Allan Lake

Alfred Lake

LAKE ATWOOD

Map 12 ↑

Map 17 ↑

Map 17 ↓

Ramp, Geminis, and Pyramid, from Atwood

Ramp Peak and First Gemini, view from Trail Rider Pass

First Gemini, from Ramp Peak

One-way Route Summary

Reference	Miles	Gain/Loss	Time Est.	Class
Map 15 or 16	1.0	-360'/+500'	30 min	1+

First Gemini, the highest of the Geminis, is a very easy, quick climb from Ramp Peak. It's just under a mile to the north of Ramp on undemanding terrain, and the route is obvious. Most of the distance is on a broad, almost plateaulike ridge. At the low point of the route (the saddle area at M15.5 and M16.3), you'll still be at more than twelve thousand feet. In spite of the harsh altitude, this area is strikingly peaceful and is even dotted with white clustered flowers (Smelowskia) in early season.

As you climb closer to the summit of First Gemini, you'll have to do a little boulder-hopping, but it's still easy (CL 1+). As you climb, be sure to look at the east face. It's an absolutely massive conglomeration of chutes and buttresses. In some places, looking directly down the vertical and overhung cliffs, you lose sight of the bottom. Of course, there's some exposure being above the cliffs, but it's very easy to stay away from.

Anders Clark hikes toward First Gemini (right) and Second Gemini (left)

Second Gemini, from First Gemini

One-way Route Summary

Reference	Miles	Gain/Loss	Time Est.	Class
Map 15 or 16	0.6	-165'/+85'	30 min	2 or 3+

After experiencing the mild climb to First Gemini, and looking at the small elevation change going northwest along the ridge to Second Gemini, you'd think this route would be similar. But it has some pleasant surprises. At first you'll be hopping along on piles of wobbly, flat rocks, about what you'd expect. Then, starting at about the midpoint between the two, you'll come to a fascinating area of stacked rocks and rock strata. The ridge is completely broken up into tall blocks, cracks, and large crevices you can scramble through, creating a mazelike path, a sort of obstacle course. Narrow and flat rocks randomly span the cracks and crevices, balanced across the openings, bringing to mind Stonehenge. Picking your way directly through and over the more interesting parts requires some fun Class 3+ climbing and scrambling. Alas, the area is quite short and ends all too quickly. If you're pressed for time, or maybe on the way back, you could easily bypass this rough area by traversing beneath the ridge top. You'll find an easygoing slope by descending about fifty feet to the south of

The ridge to Second Gemini from First Gemini

the ridge. This slope (CL 2) has intermittent, level pathlike areas that you can follow until you're beneath the summit of Second Gemini.

Second Gemini Descent to East Timothy Lake

One-way Route Summary

Reference	Miles	Gain/Loss	Time Est.	Class
Map 15	4.2	-2,285′	2.5-3 hrs	2

For the return trip to East Timothy Lake from Second Gemini, you can cut beneath First Gemini (on CL 2 slopes) instead of going over the summit. Upon reaching the saddle area (M15.5), continue south across the flats (CL 1+) beneath Ramp Peak to the "edge" of Ramp's southern slopes. You can descend anywhere on Ramp's southern slopes, but the route indicated on the maps is still the ideal way (a bit less rough and steep, with fast boulder-hopping).

ALTERNATIVE DESCENT

One tempting route, looking at map contour lines, is the southwestern ridge of Ramp Peak. In reality, it is a jagged ridge for most of the way. However, it's generally stable with colorful boulders and provides some additional views and "interesting" climbing variety. From the saddle (M15.6), you can descend a very steep slope (CL 2+ to 3) to the Rampway. This route is slightly longer than going down Ramp's southern slopes, and will probably take an extra twenty minutes or so.

Pyramid Peak, from East Timothy Lake

One-way Route Summary

Reference	Miles	Gain/Loss	Time Est.	Class
Map 15, P1	3.6	+2,265′	2-2.5 hrs	3+

The first part of this route ascends a half-mile-wide bench or ramp that circles at the head of the Swift Creek basin (see Map 15). It's a simple route, but further details are in the "Ramp Peak, from East Timothy Lake" description. At the top of the bench (M15.3), the route splits: one climbs to Ramp Peak, the other to the saddle (M15.4) between Ramp and Pyramid Peaks.

Begin climbing northeast up to the Ramp-Pyramid saddle. To avoid the steeper, more unstable boulders directly beneath the saddle, make a long zigzag path by angling up Ramp Peak's moderate (CL 2) slopes, then cutting back across to the saddle. Nearing

North face and west ridge of Pyramid Peak

the top of the saddle, there are some enormous boulders that are fun to climb on. From the saddle, the route follows Pyramid's rough ridge to the summit. Jump to "Pyramid Peak, the West Ridge" description for details.

Pyramid Peak, from Ramp Peak

One-way Route Summary

Reference	Miles	Gain/Loss	Time Est.	Class
Map 15 or 16	1.0	-505'/+545'	1.5 hrs	2+ or 3+

This route follows the ridgeline from Ramp Peak to Pyramid Peak. It drops southeast from the summit of Ramp to a saddle (M15.4 and M16.4), and then climbs Pyramid's west ridge.

Much of the route down to the saddle consists of average boulder-hopping on large, flat rocks. Just off the summit, there's a short Class 2+ section, but with relatively stable boulders. Afterward the angle lessens considerably, and you'll be descending moderate Class 2 terrain until nearing the saddle, where it gets rougher again. The descent to the saddle is uneventful and easy compared to climbing Pyramid's west ridge, where you'll spend most of your time. Read "Pyramid Peak, the West Ridge" for details.

Pyramid Peak, the West Ridge

One-way Route Summary

Reference	Miles	Gain/Loss	Time Est.	Class
Map 15 or 16	0.6	+545	45 min	3+

Pyramid's west ridge is a short but intense climb involving some fun scrambles above Pyramid's fabulous north-face headwall. From the saddle, the headwall is stunning. It rises vertically for about three hundred feet, with contrasting light-colored and reddish rock layers cut smoothly off in a concave fashion by glaciers.

The route begins at the saddle (M15.4 and M16.4) between Ramp and Pyramid. The saddle is basically a rough assortment of flat platelike rocks. As you climb up the first half of the ridge (CL 2 to 3), you'll find that often the ridge top is the most stable, with less incline than the side slope, but be cautious as it's very exposed with the headwall directly beneath.

At about the midpoint there's an overhung, blocky knob. Climbing around the knob and getting back on the ridge, you'll come to a fifty-foot-long smooth, level area, certainly uncharacteristic for the ridge. Just afterward, there's a thick, stubby, crumbling pinnacle that seems ready to topple over. The most natural route goes right underneath it, which is a bit unsettling.

After the pinnacle, the ridge top before the summit turns quite rough. It has stacks and jumbled mounds of rock—Class 3 or 3+—but it's easier

Dennis Clark climbs the west ridge of Pyramid Peak

(CL 2+) if you climb well below the ridge top. The summit is small and has a fantastic view of the high, wild Kings-Emmons ridge, consisting of a series of 13ers leading to Kings Peak.

If you're headed back down the northwest ridge to the Pyramid-Ramp saddle, plan on about the same time it took you to make the ascent.

Pyramid Peak Descent to Atwood Basin

One-way Route Summary

Reference	Miles	Gain/Loss	Time Est.	Class
Map 16	2.7	-2,265'	2 hrs	2 or 2+

To make a direct descent to the Atwood Basin, you can follow the eastern ridge of Pyramid. This would also be a good way to climb Pyramid from Atwood if you needed to do it separate from Ramp Peak. There are no cliffs or tricky route-finding, so reversing these directions shouldn't be a problem.

In early summer, you'll probably find a long snowfield along the first half mile of this ridge (ending at M16.5). If conditions are right, you can make a very quick descent by glissading or slide-stepping down. Just off the summit, the ridge angle is steep (CL 2 or 2+ if you're on boulders), but it quickly eases

East ridge of Pyramid Peak

off to moderate or mild angles (CL 2 boulders), so it'll be a fast descent whether you're on boulders or snow.

The easygoing ridge ends at a cliffy, rugged face (M16.5). From there, turn left, descending the bouldered northern slope. The slope averages Class 2, maybe 2+, with generally stable boulders made more difficult because you're descending. The boulders don't last long—after twenty minutes or so, about halfway down the slope, the boulder field ends at a lower-angle vegetated area. Except for a short strip of boulders, you can walk on this vegetation down the rest of the slope. Stay to the left to avoid a big boulder field on the ridge's shoulder near the bottom (M16.6). The two lakes just south of Lake George Beard and surrounding meadows create some beautiful scenery.

To reach the Lake Atwood area, head east down a swale or gully. The bottom of the gully tends to be rocky and choked with shrubs, but you can stay up on the north (left) side on grass and consolidated rocky soil.

There's a huge moraine and boulder field (M16.7) that extends from the western shores of Lake Atwood up to Pyramid's east face. When you arrive at Lake Atwood, you can follow the shoreline, climbing over the moraine's boulders. There's a short, steep, eroding bulge at the southern end; otherwise, this route is similar to going across the top of the moraine. After this, the boulder-hopping is finally over, and you'll have an easy walk back to camp (a long walk, though, if you're going to the east end of Lake Atwood).

Summit of Mount Emmons

Mount Emmons, from Atwood Basin

One-way Route Summary

Reference	Miles	Gain/Loss	Time Est.	Class
Map 17, P1	3.0	+2,420'	2-2.5 hrs	2

This route goes up Mount Emmons's curved, wide, and relatively gentle northern ridge. From Mount Emmons, you can complete the Emmons Loop by continuing to Glacier Peak and Pinnacle Peak, and descending Pinnacle to the Atwood Basin.

The route is obvious—it's the easiest-looking direct route up Emmons's northern side. From the Lake Atwood area, walk south across the basin to the base of the ridge (M17.2), passing by the west side of Allred and Allen Lakes. The base of the ridge is very spread out, and you can start up anywhere due south of Allen Lake (but avoid starting up from Carrot Lake).

The first part of the ridge is initially consolidated or partially vegetated with early summer bright-yellow flowers and has easy, fast hiking (CL 1 to 1+). Stick to the edge (the highest part) of the ridge (M17.3), where you'll see superb views of Carrot Lake.

The easygoing terrain ends rather abruptly, and you'll start climbing up an average Class 2 boulder slope. It has the occasional shifty rock, but is generally

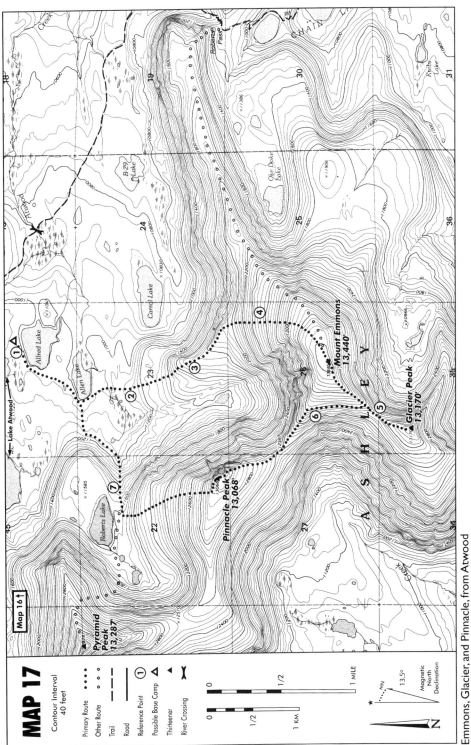

MAP 17

Contour Interval
40 feet

Primary Route	••••
Other Route	○ ○ ○
Trail	– – –
Road	——
Reference Point	①
Possible Base Camp	△
Thirteener	▲
River Crossing	✕

Map 16 ↑

0   1/2   1 MILE

0   1/2   1 KM

N

13.5°
MN
Magnetic
North
Declination

Pyramid
Peak
13,287

Pinnacle Peak
13,068

Mount Emmons
13,440

Glacier Peak
13,170

A S H L E Y   V A L L E Y

Emmons, Glacier, and Pinnacle, from Atwood

quite stable, at a moderate slope angle. In about twenty minutes, you'll reach a bench of sorts, where the slope angle eases up and you can walk up intermittent vegetated patches (M17.4) for a short distance.

The boulders start up again, and the slope gets a little steeper (CL 2). You can take almost any route up the wide face; it's all about the same difficulty and slope angle. Just keep climbing directly upward more or less toward the summit ridgeline.

The slope angle gradually lessens as the ridge narrows and curves west toward the summit. When the ridge turns almost flat (CL 1), the summit is just minutes away. Although the ridge has narrowed, it is still so broad that you won't see the south-side view unless you make it a point to walk to the southern edge.

A cairn and a 1962 USGS marker denote the high point. In the past, this summit has had a register. Mount Emmons undoubtedly has the most expansive summit of all the 13ers—it's basically level for a remarkable quarter mile going east to west and blocks most of the view into the basins below.

Mount Emmons, from Pinnacle Peak

One-way Route Summary

Reference	Miles	Gain/Loss	Time Est.	Class
Map 18	1.2	-480'/+855'	1 hr	2+

From Pinnacle Peak, you'll simply be following the ridge top southeast to the summit of Mount Emmons. The route is moderate and very straightforward, but Mount Emmons is a massive peak that stretches well beyond what you can see, so it takes longer than you might expect.

Coming off Pinnacle Peak, you'll climb down through a short, average Class 2 section. The rest of the descent will be quick (CL 1+) on flat-lying rocks. You'll end up at a very wide, gentle saddle with patchy vegetation. This saddle is marked on maps with USGS elevation point 12587.

Shortly after leaving the saddle on the ascent up Emmons's ridge, you'll come to a rougher area, a small bulge in the ridge (a short-lived CL 2+). The return route from the Emmons-Glacier saddle meets up just above this area (M18.4). For another twenty minutes or so, you'll climb very average Class 2 boulder slopes, after which the slope angle lessens considerably. The slope will eventually level out onto a very broad, bouldered plateau. The highest point is just several more minutes along the rocky flats, denoted by a cairn and a 1962 USGS marker.

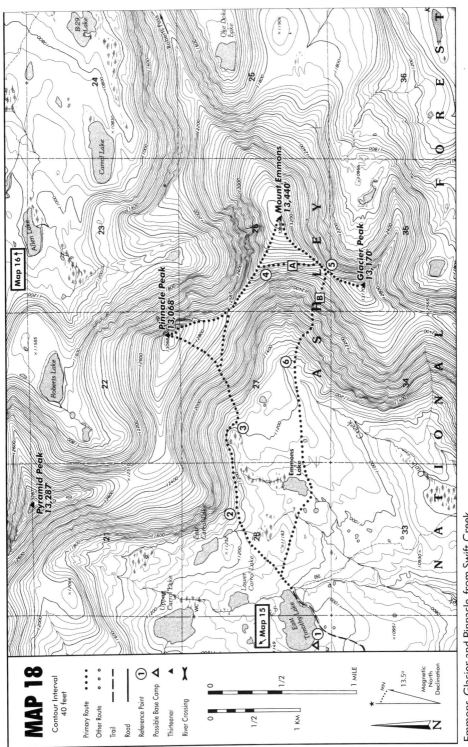

Emmons, Glacier, and Pinnacle, from Swift Creek

Mount Emmons and Glacier Peak, view from East Timothy Lake

Glacier Peak, from Mount Emmons

One-way Route Summary

Reference	Miles	Gain/Loss	Time Est.	Class
Maps 17 and 18	0.8	-540'/+270'	30-45 min	2

The ridge from Emmons to Glacier Peak is a short, relatively fast route. In the process of "climbing" Glacier Peak, you'll lose twice as much elevation as you gain.

Descending to the southwest from Emmons, you'll go over sections of flat, wobbly boulders (average CL 2). Stay near the edge of the ridge for the easiest descent. The ridge turns into a gentle, consolidated saddle (M18.5 and M17.5). You should see a snowfield on the east side of the saddle (likely year-round).

Glacier Peak, view from Mount Emmons's southwest ridge

From the saddle, the climb to the summit of Glacier will be quick—about fifteen to twenty minutes, less time than the descent from Emmons—and fairly easy (CL 1+ to 2). The ridge crest has some rougher, larger boulder-hopping. Staying off the ridge to the right (west), the route is faster, with stable, smaller boulders, rocks, and even some soil.

On the summit of Glacier Peak, you'll see many rocks where one side is smooth, flat, and striated—strong evidence of glacial activity. Directly off the east side of the summit are some vertical and overhung rock faces, with large areas of similar appearance.

See page 152 for the "Pinnacle Peak, from Glacier Peak" route.

Glacier Peak Descent to East Timothy Lake

One-way Route Summary

Reference	Miles	Gain/Loss	Time Est.	Class
Map 18, Route A	3.5	-2,150′	2 hrs	2+

This is the final part of the Emmons Loop that started from East Timothy Lake (M18.1). The best option for the descent is to use your ascent route, except cutting across the faces of Emmons and Pinnacle instead of reclimbing them (Route A). You can see the whole route from the summit of Glacier.

Descend Glacier Peak back to the Glacier-Emmons saddle (about ten minutes) (M18.5). Walk up the smooth saddle until meeting the start of Emmons boulders, then make a straight traverse north across the face of Emmons (CL 2+, about twenty minutes). If you stay high—slightly above the Glacier-Emmons saddle level—you'll avoid cliffy slide areas below and stay on lower-angled slopes. You'll probably even catch some terracelike sections along the way, but the boulders are a bit wobbly, and going horizontally makes it harder. When you've reached Emmons's northwest ridge (M18.4), climb down to the Emmons-Pinnacle saddle. Then make another traverse, this time slightly descending across the moderate slopes of Pinnacle until intersecting your original ascent route.

ALTERNATIVE DESCENT TO EAST TIMOTHY LAKE (ROUTE B): 3.1 MILES, CLASS 3+, 2.5 HOURS

This route is tempting because you can see the basin below and don't have to backtrack. It's about a half mile shorter and will take roughly the same amount of time as Route A. However, it has a wearying and somewhat hazardous midsection consisting of loose rock and unstable boulders.

From the Glacier-Emmons saddle (M18.5), start descending directly downslope. The first twenty minutes aren't too bad (CL 2). However, the trail soon deteriorates into steep, unstable terrain with loose boulders or slide gullies (CL 3 to 3+, for looseness). This section is slow going; it'll probably last at least thirty to forty minutes. In the worst sections, almost every step seems to require careful, focused attention. Nearing the bottom, the slope angle lessens and the stability gets better. You'll drop 1,700 feet in 0.7 miles from saddle to basin.

You'll end up in the basin at the head of Owl Creek, where the slopes of all three peaks meet (M18.6). This is a beautiful area, with large grass flats and a nice-size clear spring (the origin of Owl Creek).

Take a course directly west, passing to the south of Emmons Lake in order to avoid its northern bogs. There are some marshes on the south end of the lake as well, but you can cross the outlet stream by some small ponds. After the lake, just stay on a contouring path (or higher), and you'll eventually see East Timothy Lake. Except for a few boulder fields just after rounding Emmons Lake, it's fast Class 1+ hiking the whole way from the base of Emmons.

Pinnacle Peak, from East Timothy Lake

One-way Route Summary

Reference	Miles	Gain/Loss	Time Est.	Class
Map 18, P1	2.5	+2,045	2 hrs	3

From the Swift Creek side, Pinnacle Peak is the first of the three Emmons Loop summits. The route described here ascends directly to Pinnacle Peak and follows the ridgeline to Mount Emmons and Glacier Peak. From there, you simply return the way you came. Or you could take a harder alternative descent that drops directly down from Glacier Peak to the head of Owl Creek.

From East Timothy Lake, the goal is to climb up the bulge that extends down from Pinnacle Peak's southwest face. To get to the base of this climb and avoid bogs along the way, first take a straight course northeast to the closest point along the base of the high ridge (M18.2). It's an easy Class 1 walk through meadows.

When you reach the base of the boulder fields, contour at the edge. You'll descend slightly as you go, but resist the urge to start climbing just yet. The basin is much easier than the boulder slopes (I've done it both ways). Along the way, you'll pass above some bogs that drain into Emmons Lake. You'll reach a

Pinnacle Peak, view from Emmons-Pinnacle saddle

flat, grassy, somewhat boggy area with a scenic little meandering stream
(M18.3). The stream originates from a cloudy, silt-laden spring gushing out
from underneath the boulder slope.

The real climbing finally begins. Walk east to the end of the grassy area and
hike up the low, rounded, partially vegetated ridge. This low ridge has easy
climbing for a short distance, and then suddenly connects with steeper terrain
and large, unstable boulders. The instability makes it probably Class 3. As you
climb, keep in mind that the terrain gets steeper farther to your right (east),
turning into a system of large, crumbling cliffs that rise to the face of Emmons.
The sketchy climbing lasts only about twenty minutes. Then the angle starts to
ease up, and the boulders become more stable (CL 2 turning to CL 1+). Another half mile (or approximately thirty minutes) later, you'll be standing on
the summit of Pinnacle Peak.

As you'll notice, this summit suddenly looks less like a bump on the ridge
and more like a separate peak. In stark contrast to the rounded side you just
went up, the east face is a craggy, incredible scene with some extreme gullies
that might give you a bit of vertigo. As if for emphasis, the face also sports a
pinnacle atop a hundred-foot cliff.

Refer to page 146 for the "Mount Emmons, from Pinnacle Peak" route
description.

Pinnacle Peak, from Glacier Peak

One-way Route Summary

Reference	Miles	Gain/Loss	Time Est.	Class
Map 17, Route A	1.5	-590'/+480'	1-1.5 hrs	2+

This route is part of the Emmons Loop that started from Atwood Basin. The route cuts across the face of Emmons to its northwest ridge (Route A), then follows the ridge to the top of Pinnacle. You can see the whole route from the summit of Glacier.

Descend Glacier Peak back to the Glacier-Emmons saddle (about ten minutes) (M17.5). Walk up the smooth saddle until meeting the start of Emmons boulders, then make a straight traverse north across the face of Emmons (CL 2+, about twenty minutes). If you stay high—slightly above the Glacier-Emmons saddle level—you'll avoid cliffy slide areas below and stay on lower-angled slopes. You'll probably even catch some terracelike sections along the way, but the boulders are a bit wobbly, and going horizontally makes it harder.

When you've reached Emmons's northwest ridge (M17.6), climb down to the Emmons-Pinnacle saddle. As you descend the ridge to the saddle, there's a short rougher section; otherwise, it is average to easy. From there, start climbing the ridge to Pinnacle Peak. The ridge initially consists of patchy vegetation and soil (CL 1), then piles of flat-lying rocks, and later more typical boulders (an easy CL 2).

You will top out above a curved, massive, almost vertical cliff, hundreds of feet high, with Pinnacle's pinnacle in view below. It's really quite stunning. The high point is on the other side of the curved headwall.

Pinnacle Peak Descent to Lake Atwood

One-way Route Summary

Reference	Miles	Gain/Loss	Time Est.	Class
Map 17	2.5	-2,050'	2 hrs	2+

This is the final part of the Emmons Loop that started from Lake Atwood (M17.1). The route follows Pinnacle Peak's rounded northern slope down to the Roberts Lake bench, then drops to the east to the basin floor via a gully. It's a straightforward, fairly easy route. It will probably take just over an hour to reach the basin floor.

In early summer, you may have to negotiate a corniced line of snow that runs along Pinnacle's entire east-west ridgeline. You can go around it by walk-

Mount Emmons, view from Pinnacle Peak

ing west a half mile along the ridge, then angling back to the east somewhat as you descend (in order to reach easier slope angles). Or, immediately down from the summit, where the ridgeline drops abruptly to a new level, you may discover that the cornice has broken up, creating a doable way down a snowfield (use your best judgment).

Going downslope, the boulders are somewhat wobbly at first (CL 2+), but they quickly give way to more consolidated boulders (CL 2) with intermittent grass and soil. The vegetation patches gradually increase, making for some easy hiking (CL 1 to 1+).

On the last slope before Roberts Lake, there's a large swath of unsavory boulders that gets steeper closer to the gully (below you to the right). Conveniently, there's a mostly vegetated path that cuts right through them, approximately in line with the middle of Roberts Lake.

At Roberts Lake on the bench, cut to the right (east). You'll reach a large, V-shaped gully (M17.7). Pinnacle's boulder field tumbles down the right-side slope, but you can easily walk down the left-side slope on grassy and rocky terrain. At the bottom, contour northward around the base of the bench, going through some beautiful small meadows. Stay high to avoid marshes. After hiking up a gentle rise, you can follow small streamlet courses down to Allen Lake, and from there to Lake Atwood.

APPENDIX

Other Routes and Strategies

There are, of course, other routes you can use to climb the 13ers. The following routes are good alternatives to the routes previously presented. They are all clearly doable (no major cliffs and the like, except where noted) and within the range of difficulty of the primary routes in this book. Route information was gathered from topographic maps, other people, or personal experience. I have done some but not all of these routes. The descriptions are meant to be brief but useful tips and suggestions to point you in the right direction—nothing more, nothing less! Most of these routes are indicated on the maps by a series of open dots (circles).

TOKEWANNA PEAK

There are several common routes from the north. The first option is to hike up the Middle Fork Blacks Fork Trail. The other two approaches use the east-west Bear River Smiths Fork Trail (BRSF) to access Tokewanna's northwest and northeast ridges. Round-trip, both BRSF routes spend 10-12 total miles on above-timberline ridge crests, so thunderstorm exposure is a drawback.

Going the Middle Fork way, first drive to the West Fork Blacks Fork River bridge (see the "Driving to the Trailheads" chapter). Immediately after the bridge, go up a lesser-used dirt road, which eventually connects to the Middle Fork Trail. The trail climbs into the Middle Fork basin, where you can climb to the summit on a minor, relatively easy ridge by Bob's Lake. This route is 22 miles round-trip from the East Fork road. Refer to Maps 3 and 4.

Using the BRSF approach from the West Fork Blacks Fork side, you'd first walk up the primitive road to the BRSF trail intersection (M3.2). Head east on the trail, climb up to Tokewanna's very long northwest ridge, and walk south along the ridge to the summit. Half of the ridge is described in the "Tokewanna Peak, from West Fork Blacks Fork" route. The entire route is 15.5 miles round-trip from the Car Park. Refer to Maps 3 and 4.

Using the BRSF approach from the East Fork Blacks Fork side, drive up the East Fork road to where the BRSF crosses (again, refer to "Driving to the Trailheads"). Walk west on the BRSF trail up to the ridgetop (an extension of Tokewanna's northeast ridge), then turn south and hike along the scenic ridgetop to the summit. It is 19 miles round-trip and has more ups and downs than Tokewanna's northwest ridge. Refer to Maps 3 and 5.

Quandary Peak

You could try a more direct route on Quandary's northwest slopes, starting at M7.2. It looks less rough than other routes, but with loose and steep terrain it is probably harder work. As you climb, aim for the far east side (the left-hand side, looking up from below) of the flat portion of the ridge between Quandary and Mount Lovenia. When you arrive, start climbing up Quandary Peak's west ridge. When you reach a cliff band, walk beneath it to the left (east), and the first break you come to is the short crack (M7.7) described in the "Mount Lovenia, from Quandary Peak" section.

Wilson Peak

From Porcupine Pass on the Highline Trail, you can make an easy one-third-mile climb up a rounded ridge to the western point (M9.7) of Wilson's flat-topped ridge. Another option starts at the small lake marked with USGS elevation point 11757, just one-third of a mile above the Highline Trail. It goes directly up Wilson's southern slopes on easy-to-moderate terrain. The drawback to these routes is the long access trails and no other nearby 13ers to climb. Another route that has been suggested in other guidebooks is walking the ridge from Smiths Fork Pass, and then going up Wilson's northern ridge, but the final ridge to the summit is extremely rough; I'd definitely recommend other routes.

One of the most spectacular routes I've done is a circumambulation of Wilson Peak and Red Castle (8.5 miles, with a 2,400-foot elevation gain). You can start at any point on the Red Castle or Smiths Fork Pass trails and connect Wilson's west and east routes together (see Map 9). Except for a (sensible) shortcut between the two trails above Lower Red Castle Lake, all trails or routes have been described in Group 2 (half of the circumambulation would be done opposite to the descriptions).

Mount Powell

From the Henrys Fork basin, there are doable routes going up Powell's eastern slopes (see Map 10). The easiest of such routes starts from Henrys Fork Lake. Hike west up the lake's inlet (or nearby slopes) to the wide-open, rocky meadows where Lake Blanchard sits. Veer west-northwest toward the colossal buttress and cirque above Castle Lake. Hike into the cirque and then climb south up a moderate slope to a 13,000-foot point (M10.5) due north of Powell's highest summit.

Another way to climb Mount Powell is via Flat Top Mountain, an extension of Powell's northern ridge (see Map 8). You can climb to Flat Top by using the North Slope Highline Trail, which intersects the East Fork Smiths Fork Trail (M8.2) and the Henrys Fork Trail (M8.12, "Elkhorn Crossing"). To get to either of these trail junctions, refer to the East Fork Smiths Fork Trail and Henrys Fork Trail descriptions. The off-trail portion of the route would leave the North Slope Highline Trail at Lake Hessie, or from the ridge flats northwest of Bear Lake. Powell's summit the East Fork Smiths Fork way is 22.5 miles round-trip from the trailhead; the Henrys Fork way is 2.5 miles longer. As expected, Flat Top is a gentle ridge. Half the total distance from the trailhead is exposed, high above timberline.

Gilbert Peak

Some hikers have used the broad northern ridge of Gilbert (see Maps 8 and 11). It's a long, mostly flat ridge with average Uinta boulders, but not difficult. You can get to the ridge by walking east on the North Slope Highline Trail, which leaves the Henrys Fork Trail at Elkhorn Crossing (M8.12) (also refer to trail description). If you follow the North Slope Highline Trail exactly (the U turn after Elkhorn Crossing), Gilbert is 21 miles round-trip from the Henrys Fork Trailhead; otherwise, it's 17.5 miles. Another approach, a solitary route that few (if any) people use, starts from Gilbert Creek southeast of Gilbert Peak.

Gunsight Peak

You can climb Gunsight Peak by climbing directly up the ridge from Gunsight Pass (see Map 11), but it's a rough route. From the top of Gunsight Pass, head northeast along the ridge, going up and over the first bump. From there you'll encounter some huge cliffs. You can traverse around them to the right and then head directly up to the summit on very steep and loose talus and boulders. The route from Dollar Lake is much easier.

Kings Peak and South Kings Peak

Anderson Pass is by far the easiest route to Kings and South Kings, but if you'd like more of a challenge or would like more solitude, try climbing them from the east (see Maps 12 and 16). The eastern routes make the most sense when approached via the Atwood Basin Trail. From the trail in Painter Basin or from Trail Rider Pass, hike up to the small unnamed lake at USGS elevation point 12302. From there you have a choice of good routes to either summit. You could climb directly up to Kings on its moderate southern slopes or eastern ridge. Or you could climb to the saddle between Kings and South Kings. A good-looking route to South Kings goes up a small spur ridge southeast of the summit. The ridge from Second Gemini to South Kings is also very doable but is a longer access.

Fortress Peak

One possibility goes directly up the southern slopes of Fortress from the Highline Trail west of Anderson Pass (see Map 12). The route starts at the beginning of the final switchback (the tenth, counting from the bottom). It follows a loose and steep talus slope between two cliff bands to the summit. I wouldn't choose it over the eastern ridge route, but it is certainly more direct.

Pyramid Peak

This moderately steep route is obvious if you look at it while descending Pinnacle Peak. You could try it for an ascent or descent. First hike up to the bench where Roberts Lake sits (see Map 17), then walk to the point where Pyramid's eastern and southern slopes meet. Climb directly upslope toward the summit, on sparse vegetation and generally consolidated terrain. At the halfway point, veer to the right in order to stay on easier slopes (still vegetated and consolidated) and connect to Pyramid's eastern ridge route.

First and Second Geminis

The best routes to the Geminis go over other summits, namely, either Ramp Peak or South Kings Peak (see Map 15 or 16). The cliffy east side of the Geminis is out of the question, and the west side is very rugged and far from any trail. It's interesting to note that the round-trip distance and cumulative elevation gain are approximately the same whether you reach the Geminis from Anderson Pass or from Upper Carrol Lake (Swift Creek drainage). The difference is that the ridge route from Anderson Pass is considerably rougher than the route from Swift Creek and Ramp Peak. Also, if you're hiking from a base camp in the Yellowstone or Henrys Fork drainage (which is quite likely), you'll end up adding many more miles to the trip and huge elevation gain. So going over South Kings Peak to the Geminis is certainly doable, but the Ramp Peak approach to the Geminis remains the overall best choice.

Mount Emmons

Emmons has possibilities from the south and east (see Map 17). One good route starts at Roberts Pass and follows Emmons's very long, easygoing eastern ridge all the way to the summit (2.6 miles, +2,300 feet one-way). There's a short, steep climb to the ridge from Roberts Pass (no cliffs involved) and a moderately rough section halfway up the summit slope, but overall it's a straightforward, relatively easy route. This would be a good choice from the Chain Lakes area. This route to Emmons is 27 miles round-trip from the Uinta Trailhead.

One-Day Round-Trips from the Trailheads

Except for a few summits, one-day trips are reserved for the ultrafit who can hike twenty to thirty or more miles a day with thousands of feet in elevation gain—not your average hiker! To lessen the miles, you'd want to take the most direct route possible, and the more of the route that is on trails, the better. These same concerns actually apply to high-mileage overnight trips as well.

With only minor changes (like shortcuts across meadows), most of the primary routes described in this book would work well. There are some exceptions, and some of these shorter route options are explained as "Other Routes" above. Another route consideration is whether to go over another summit using a connecting ridge or choose another way.

At the beginning of each Group chapter, look at the "Round-Trip Routes" table. You will see that Tokewanna Peak is actually quite doable, at fourteen miles round-trip from the West Fork Blacks Fork Car Park (M3.1). Peaks that are close to twenty miles round-trip from the trailhead are Gilbert, Gunsight, and Dome (from Henrys Fork), and Quandary and Wasatch (from East Fork

Blacks Fork). Gilbert and Gunsight are also good candidates because the terrain is relatively easy.

Keep in mind that in the Uintas, big elevation changes on rough terrain make a pure distance calculation less useful. Hence, trails that take you to high passes are an advantage, like the trail to Anderson Pass (the highest pass in the Uintas). Anderson Pass provides unusually quick access to several summits, including Kings Peak. Kings Peak is about 24.5 miles round-trip from Henrys Fork.

Consolidated Snow Climbs

Discussing climbing on consolidated snow in detail is beyond the realm of this book, but there are some definite advantages that you should be aware of.

During March, April, and May, firm, smooth snow creates veritable highways to the summits, making most routes easier. Instead of negotiating slow-going boulder fields, you can ski, climb, or glissade your way on consolidated snow to and from the summits, thus taking less time and effort. This makes the idea of one-day summits much more reasonable. It's a wondrous time of the year to go, having the appearance of winter, but without the short daylight hours and bitter temperatures. Other benefits: no bugs, no bogs, and you'll have the Uintas completely to yourself. Of course, you should obviously have proper equipment (including an ice axe for self-arrest) and appropriate training.

However, trailhead access is a problem due to the snowpack. One of the best access points is the Henrys Fork Trailhead (to Kings Peak–area summits). There's a plowed road from Lonetree, Wyoming, to an oil field just three miles from the trailhead. On the south slope, there's a road plowed to Yellowstone Ranch, four miles away from the Swift Creek Trailhead. Higher-elevation trailheads like Henrys Fork have a big advantage in that you won't have to hike as far to get to "good" snow.

Incidentally, the Wasatch Mountain Club makes a one-day consolidated snow climb of Kings Peak every year at the end of March. See "Information and Resources" on page 165 for contact information.

Low-Impact Wilderness Travel

In the wilderness, humans are temporary visitors, and the goal is that human impact is wholly unnoticeable except for trails. Yet hundreds of visitors leave their footprints in the often-fragile landscape. The only solution is to practice techniques that allow us to enjoy the wilderness without destroying it. Ground plants above treeline are especially vulnerable. All routes in this book pass through the alpine zone. Stay on trails as long as possible. If you must walk over tundra with a group of people, spread out over a wide area to minimize the impact. Avoid camping on tundra plants.

CAMPSITE SELECTION

Two good methods of campsite selection that treat the land lightly are using existing sites and dispersed camping. When you use existing sites (that is, bare ground), the idea is that damage has already been done. Dispersed camping is the practice of camping far away from existing sites and high-use areas. The idea is that no single camping spot is used so long that it causes lasting damage. As a side benefit, you'll also enjoy more solitude. Even with dispersed camping, you should camp on bare ground or dry grass if available. If you must camp on fragile alpine vegetation, move your camp daily or take down your tent during the day so vegetation has a chance to recover.

LEAVE NO TRACE

Leave No Trace (LNT) (see "Useful Websites" below) is a national nonprofit organization that educates about responsible use of the outdoors. The list that follows is based on LNT principles. They're recommendations, things you can do to help reduce impact to fragile alpine environments.

Plan Ahead and Prepare
- Know the regulations and special concerns for the area you'll visit.
- Prepare for extreme weather, hazards, and emergencies.
- Schedule your trip to avoid times of high use.
- Visit in small groups. Split larger parties into groups of four to six.
- Repackage food to minimize waste.
- Use a map and compass to eliminate the use of marking paint, rock cairns, or flagging.

Travel and Camp on Durable Surfaces
- Durable surfaces include established trails and campsites, rock, gravel, dry grasses, or snow.
- Protect riparian areas by camping at least two hundred feet (seventy adult steps) from lakes and streams.
- Good campsites are found, not made. Altering a site is not necessary.
- In popular areas: Use existing trails and campsites. Walk single file in the

middle of the trail, even when wet or muddy. Keep campsites small. Focus activity in areas where vegetation is absent.

- In pristine areas: Disperse use to prevent the creation of campsites and trails. Move campsites frequently. Avoid places where impacts are just beginning. When traveling cross-country, spread out across the terrain and choose the most durable surfaces.

Dispose of Waste Properly
- Pack it in, pack it out. Inspect your campsite and rest areas for trash or spilled foods. Pack out all trash, leftover food, and litter.
- Deposit solid human waste in "catholes" dug six to eight inches deep at least two hundred feet from water, camp, and trails. Pack out toilet paper or thoroughly and carefully burn it. Cover and disguise the cathole when finished.
- Even "biodegradable" soap can pollute. Use in small amounts, two hundred feet away from water sources, never in lakes or streams. Scatter strained dishwater.

Leave What You Find
- Preserve the past. Examine, but do not touch, cultural or historical structures and artifacts.
- Leave rocks, plants, and other natural objects as you found them.
- Avoid introducing or transporting nonnative species.
- Do not build structures or furniture or dig trenches.

Minimize Campfire Impacts
- Campfires can cause lasting impacts to the backcountry. Use a lightweight stove for cooking and enjoy a candle lantern for light.
- Where fires are permitted, use established fire rings, fire pans, or mound fires.
- Keep fires small. Only use sticks from the ground that can be broken by hand.
- Burn all wood and coals to ash, put out campfires completely, then scatter cool ashes.

Respect Wildlife
- Observe wildlife from a distance. Do not follow or approach.
- Never feed animals. Feeding wildlife damages their health, alters natural behaviors, and exposes them to predators and other dangers.

- Protect wildlife and your food by storing rations and trash securely.
- Control pets at all times or leave them at home.
- Avoid wildlife during sensitive times: when they are mating, nesting, and raising their young and during the winter.

Be Considerate of Other Visitors
- Respect other visitors and protect the quality of their experience.
- Be courteous. Yield to other users on the trail.
- Step to the downhill side of the trail when encountering pack stock.
- Take breaks and camp away from trails and other visitors.
- Let nature's sounds prevail. Avoid loud voices and noises.

Information and Resources

Ashley National Forest
SUPERVISOR'S OFFICE ADDRESS: 353 N. Vernal Avenue, Vernal, UT 84078
PHONE: 1-435-789-1181
WEBSITE: www.fs.fed.us/r4/ashley

Swift Creek, Yellowstone Creek, and Atwood Basin
ADDRESS: Duchesne/Roosevelt Ranger District, 650 West Highway 40
(P.O. Box 127), Roosevelt, UT 84066 or 85 West Main (P.O. Box 981),
Duchesne, UT 84021
PHONE: 1-435-722-5018 or 1-435-738-2482

Wasatch-Cache National Forest
SUPERVISOR'S OFFICE ADDRESS: 8226 Federal Building, 125 South State Street,
Salt Lake City, UT 84138
PHONE: 1-801-524-3900
WEBSITE: www.fs.fed.us/wcnf

Bear River and Blacks Fork
ADDRESS: Evanston Ranger District, 1565 Highway 150, Suite A (P.O. Box 1880),
Evanston, WY 82930
PHONE: 1-307-789-3194

Smiths Fork and Henrys Fork
ADDRESS: Mountain View Ranger District, 321 Highway 414 (P.O. Box 129),
Mountain View, WY 82939
PHONE: 1-307-782-6555

Topographic Maps

iGage Mapping Corporation

Sells USGS topographic maps on CD-ROM (every 7.5", 1:100,000- and 1:250,000-scale map for every state), via outdoor and map retailers.

ADDRESS (CORPORATE): 1545 South 1100 East #3, Salt Lake City, UT 84105

PHONE: 1-801-412-0011 or 1-888-450-4922

WEBSITE: www.igage.com or www.alltopo.com

Natural Resources Map and Bookstore

Official outlet for U.S. Geological Survey publications and maps; also carries a variety of books for recreational activities in Utah.

ADDRESS: 1594 West North Temple, Salt Lake City, UT 84114-6100

PHONE: 1-801-537-3320 or 1-888-UTAHMAP

WEBSITE: mapstore.utah.gov

REI (Recreation Equipment Inc.)

ADDRESS: 3285 East 3300 South, Salt Lake City, UT 84109

PHONE: 1-801-486-2100

WEBSITE: www.rei.com

U.S. Geological Survey

ADDRESS: Box 25046, Federal Center, Denver, CO 80225

PHONE: 1-303-236-5900 or 1-888-ASK-USGS (1-888-275-8747)

WEBSITE: www.usgs.gov

Utah Idaho Map World

ADDRESS: 6562 South State Street, Murray, UT 84107. They also have other locations along the Wasatch Front.

PHONE: 1-801-307-5555

Other Resources

Wasatch Mountain Club

ADDRESS: 1390 South 1100 E., Suite 103, Salt Lake City, UT 84105

PHONE: 1-801-463-9842

WEBSITE: www.wasatchmountainclub.org

www.americasroof.com: guide to high points of all kinds in the United States

www.fs.fed.us: U.S. National Forest website with links to all national forests

www.gorp.com: a very large website with outdoor information (trails, wildernesses, parks, and the like)

www.highpointers.org: Highpointers Club website, with information on the fifty state summits

www.hupc.org: High Uintas Preservation Council

www.Lnt.org: Leave No Trace, a national nonprofit organization that educates about responsible use of outdoors. Also reached via 1-800-332-4100.

www.mapcard.com: customize and print maps yourself

www.mytopo.com: topographic map print-on-demand service

www.peakware.com: an online encyclopedia of the world's mountains

www.topozone.com: interactive topographic map of the United States

www.utahwild.com: information on backcountry wilderness recreation in Utah

www.weather.com and www.intellicast.com: weather forecasts

www.wilderness.org: official website of the Wilderness Society

www.wildlife.utah.gov: Utah Division of Wildlife Resources, with information on bear safety, cougars, hunting seasons, and so on

www.wrh.noaa.gov/saltlake: Utah weather forecasts from the National Weather Service

Selected Readings

Allen, Steve. *Canyoneering*. Salt Lake City: University of Utah Press, 1992.

Davis, Mel, and John Veranth. *High Uinta Trails*. Salt Lake City: Wasatch Publishers, 1998. (University of Utah Press)

Fletcher, Colin. *The Complete Walker IV*. New York: Knopf, 2002.

Graydon, Don, and Kurt Hanson. *Mountaineering: The Freedom of the Hills*. Seattle: Mountaineers, 1997.

Holmes, Don W. *Highpoints of the United States*. Salt Lake City: University of Utah Press, 2000.

Jardine, Ray. *Beyond Backpacking: Ray Jardine's Guide to Lightweight Hiking*. LaPine, Oreg.: AdventureLore Press, 1999.

Kelsey, Michael R. *Utah Mountaineering Guide*. Provo, Utah: Kelsey Publishing, 1997.

Roach, Gerry. *Colorado's Fourteeners*. Golden, Colo.: Fulcrum Publishing, 1999.

Stokes, William L. *Geology of Utah*. Salt Lake City: Utah Museum of Natural History and Utah Geological and Mineral Survey, 1986.

Veranth, John. *Hiking the Wasatch*. Salt Lake City: Wasatch Mountain Club and Wasatch Publishers, 1998. (University of Utah Press)

Weibel, Michael R., and Dan Miller. *High in Utah*. Salt Lake City: University of Utah Press, 1999.

ACKNOWLEDGMENTS

First and foremost, I'd like to thank my wife, Amy, for her support. She often sacrificed her time and assumed extra responsibilities so I could work on this project.

I'd like to recognize several Clarks. Valerie Clark has always encouraged and supported my outdoor and nature photography ambitions. She and her husband, Dennis Clark, backpacked into the basins for the majority of my Uinta trips. Cody Clark has always been a trusted and willing expedition partner over the years, although scheduling prevented him from coming on many 13er climbs. Dennis and Anders Clark climbed at least half of the twenty-one summits, most of them during the reclimbing of peaks around Mount Emmons and Kings Peak.

Ray Overson eagerly took time off work to climb all the peaks in the East Fork Blacks Fork drainage, as well as the Atwood Basin routes on another trip. Anders Clark and Kevin Thurman climbed Gilbert, Dome, and Gunsight with me over a weekend. And adept mountaineer Brent DeHaan joined me for a quick last-of-season overnight trip to Quandary Peak.

I want to acknowledge the reviewers, editors, designers, and others who helped get this book to press, though I obviously can't name everyone involved. Valerie Clark and Cody Clark volunteered to review my initial material. Dan Miller, coauthor of *High in Utah*, and Rob Jones, director of the University of Utah Outdoor Recreation Program, gave valuable reviews and suggestions, and Annette Wenda worked to produce a quality copyedit of the final manuscript. Finally, credit goes to Jeff Grathwohl at the University of Utah Press for his efforts and expertise throughout the entire publishing process.

DAVID ROSE is a hiker, backcountry skier, climber, and nature photographer who supports these delights by working as a web programmer. He is a Utah native who has lived in red rock country and along the Wasatch front. In addition to climbing all of Utah's 13ers, he has climbed the highest peak in every Utah county, hiked the Great Western Trail through Utah twice, and also backpacked through the Sierra Nevada and the Cascades on the Pacific Crest Trail. He operates websites on Utah's outdoors (www.utahwild.com) and his nature photography (www.davidrosephoto.com), among others. He currently lives in Tooele with his wife, Amy, and two children, Benjamin and Lauren.

UTAH THIRTEENERS ONLINE

For additional information and resources, visit www.utahthirteeners.com. Sign the online summit register, browse color photos, read route updates, get current website addresses, and more. You may also submit suggestions, comments, or corrections using the website.

Please send any offline correspondence to David Rose, c/o The University of Utah Press, 1795 E. South Campus Drive, Suite 101, Salt Lake City, UT 84112-9402.